I Can, I Will, I Must

Buying the Hamptons
Building a Successful Future
Becoming the Best You Can Be

Alan Schnurman

&

Eric Feil

Attitude = Altitude

Best,

Alan Schnurman

This edition published by Sagg Main Press, LLC

First Edition

Title: I Can, I Will, I Must/Alan Schnurman and Eric Feil—1st ed.

ISBN 978-1-7330165-0-6 (softcover)

Cover & Book Design by Genevieve Horsburgh

To my wife, Judy, my children, Michele and David, and my five grandchildren—Max, Eli, Leila, Joshua and Jonah. May light shine upon you and light your path…

For Tina and Sammi.
Give every day the chance
to become the most beautiful of your life.

CONTENTS

I Can, I Will, I Must

Acknowledgements

Alan Schnurman

I didn't wake up 73 years later and find myself in the future like Rip Van Winkle. I had a lot of help on the way. In Chapter 21, "Picking Your Partners," you will find one of the most important parts of a successful professional and personal life. Here are some of the partners I owe my good fortune to. Each one exemplifies TEEC—Trustworthy, Ethical, Experienced, Credible.

First is my co-author, Eric Feil, whose attitude, smile and experience have taken my story and put it to print for you to read. I cannot thank Eric enough.

Ben Zalman—My law and real estate partner for over 45 years. One of the nicest and wisest persons I know. He taught me how to be a better person.

Gary Seff, Fountainhead Construction—Could not ask for a more experienced individual in building, one who has an incredible work ethic and who is as nice as he is experienced.

Asher Bernstein, Bernstein Real Estate—Third generation of a real estate family. Experienced, Knowledgeable, Always there with the right answer. A good friend and the person you always want on your side of the table.

Jack and Gusty Folks—Their mere names bring a smile to my face. Smart, hard working, generous, what more can I say? I want to be them in my next life.

Nat Sabari—Has been my partner for almost 35 years. We met when he tiled a bathroom of my house. We've been partners ever since.

Andrew Siben, of the Siben & Siben Law Firm—My real estate psychologist. Yes, I have a real estate psychologist.

Andrew and Colleen Saunders, Saunders & Associates—It's a pleasure to work with them. They are smart, kind and thoughtful, always looking to help you in any way they can.

Paul Pepe—"The smartest guy in the room." I thank Paul for his sage advice over the years.

Avi Stein—One of the brightest businessman I know. He taught me a lot.

Irwin Blitt—My banker, friend and advisor. I will always remember Irwin's smile and his expression "I'll do the deal."

Steve and Lillian Greenberg—Friends and partners for over 50 years. Thank you both for your enduring confidence in me.

Marty Rabin and his wife Tammy Rudnick—I met Marty in our sophomore year of high school, one of the luckiest days of my life. Our road together has been blessed.

Ed Milstein and Jay Dankner—Lawyers, friends, partners—thank you for your faith in me.

Mickey Trachtenberg—He always thought I was smarter than I am.

My daughter, Michele, for her insightful comments and being there to lend a helping hand. My son, David, who was always there to listen and advise while working on his own inspirational book, *The Fast Forward Mindset*. Most of all, I want to thank them for giving me five beautiful grandchildren.

And last but not least, I would like to thank my wonderful wife, Judy, for over 50 years of love, devotion and friendship, and her keen eye for the written word.

I have always dealt through consensus—many is always better than one. Teamwork makes the dream work.

Acknowledgements

Eric Feil

"I think I'd make an interesting story."

The first time I met Alan, we were at a cocktail reception for the Hamptons real estate magazine *Behind the Hedges* in 2014. The room was filled with players from one of the world's most exclusive real estate markets, many of them faces you'd recognize from their decades atop national rankings of brokers. Alan was relatively new to the broker game, but you'd never know it from the informed manner of his conversation. *This guy seemed to know everything!* I remember thinking. *But he'd only been a broker for a few years. How was that possible?* I didn't have a drink that night, but I did leave the party with a buzz. That's the kind of effect Alan can have on you. His enthusiasm, his energy, they are infectious. *I think I'd make an interesting story.* When we sat down in Bridgehampton for our first lunch together a few weeks later, the truth of those seven words began to ring truer than I could have possibly imagined.

When Alan and I decided to collaborate on *I Can, I Will, I Must*, the title was written before anything else. It is Alan's mantra, yes, but it would also soon become the motivating phrase I said to myself every time I opened my laptop. Of course, inspiration came from my partner on this project via more than merely those words. Every Thursday I would speak with Alan, almost without exception. A great deal of those talks formed the foundation for this book, but the full extent of them helped me see the world, and my approach to it, in a different light. It was not uncommon on those Thursdays for my wife to say, "You spoke with Alan today, didn't you?" and the implication was clear: my mood might be just a bit better, my outlook a bit sunnier, than normal. Alan, you are one of a kind, and my gratitude for your friendship and wisdom are boundless. This is, without doubt, only the start of a long journey for us.

On the subject of journeys, I am thrilled that my longtime friend and colleague Jeff Iorio, whose way with words I have long admired, was able to join me on this one. His sense of voice, skill in massaging a message and understanding of real estate provided an invaluable edit and polish. A toast to you, Jeff, if not from the top of Everest then at least from the top of the mound at Fenway Park.

Extreme thanks also go to (*if you hear that annoying awards show music starting to play in an effort to get me off the stage, ignore it*): Gen Horsburgh, for creating the cover design for *I Can, I Will, I Must*, and whose magazine layouts for stories I've written in *Behind the Hedges* and *Dan's Papers* lend them a visual element that take the storytelling to another level. Richard Burns and Dan Rattiner, who opened my door to the East End and who share a love of stories about special moments and people in Hamptons history. Gregg Camfield and Peshe Kuriloff, who back in my days at the University of Pennsylvania taught me to always keep my audience in mind as I wrote, and to have the confidence in my own voice. My friends Scott, Mike, Larry and Dave (and Rick, who was there in spirit and via text), and a fateful weekend when you helped me decide it was time to take the big step that got me to this moment.

I'm a believer that this is a world of happy accidents that can bring people together, and with that I give a special shout-out to Steve McKenna, who turned a lost wallet that was never actually lost into an introduction to Alan and a story with endless legs. For this story and countless others, may your *tarte flambée* be always hot and your classic with salt always a double, my man.

The importance of family is a topic Alan and I have discussed at length, and one we cannot underscore strongly enough. I hope all of you reading this book are lucky enough to have people who are always in your corner, there to lend a hand or an ear or an encouraging word, just as I have been…and not only throughout the writing, rewriting and editing of this project. They (whoever "they" are) say you can't choose your family, but if I could, I would pick each and every one of you:

The NYC Feils—my brother, Adam, Kitch, Jackson and Benjamin—who are a source of joy and laughter and love larger than they know.

Hank and Maryann, Cathy, Ben, Debbie, Evan, Glenn, Alison, Danielle, Leah, Sabrina, Joshua, Abigail, James, Thomas, Alex and Jason—in-laws and out-laws and so much more.

My mother, who was always my best audience and was happy I was an English major. My father, who like Alan was a people person before there was a term for such things, and whose example of work ethic drove me through those nights I pushed into the wee hours of the morning. My grandmother, probably the only person I've ever known whose positive outlook on life could give Alan a run for his money.

Tina and Sammi Gwynn, there aren't enough words, even for someone as loquacious (yes, Sammi, I just wanted to use that word) as I can be. You are, quite simply, the reason I can, I will, I must.

CHAPTER 1

I CAN, I WILL, I MUST

At 4:30 a.m. the streets of Manhattan hold promise in a way few get to see. Steam rising from manholes and shadow figures moving quickly in alleyways, deliveries made, trucks rolling and rumbling, doors locking up for the night or opening for business, dark giving way to day. There's a pulse, the city shaking off the cobwebs of sleep, a time when most of the world hasn't had a chance to do very much, or hasn't even tried.

Every day, I slip out of my East Side apartment and immerse myself in these Before Hours, among the buildings stretching skyward. I cut a solitary figure but am not alone, really. I take it all in, the people and the activity and the deals that are out there, waiting. Weather, season— they make no difference. I'm out there, every single morning. Among all the inspirational sayings that motivate me, you may be surprised to learn that the Postal Creed about neither rain nor sleet nor dark of night and so on is not among them. Torrential rains, I'm out there. Frigid winter, I'm bundled in gear worthy of Mt. Everest, out there.

In Manhattan when I'm up at 4:30 a.m. going for my walks, there's so much action. Some people are coming home from being out all night. I'm just starting my day.

I do this because I want to. And because I have to. There really is no difference between the two.

Every morning I have three quotes I say to myself, because I have to reenergize every single day. First is "I can, I will, I must." I have to say that, because to take risks, you have to be strong and you have to have confidence in yourself and your decision-making process. In short, you have to be courageous.

You also must be hopeful, have a positive outlook. Next, then, is: "Optimism is the faith that leads to achievement. Nothing can be done without hope and confidence." Helen Keller said that.

And to complete the trilogy: "Attitude equals altitude."

I've embraced these daily mantra because each quote helps me get over my own insecurities, my own doubts. The whole idea of my quote system is that it helps me break through the proverbial wall.

The approach to what I do is somewhat unique, and my CV has often veered in unusual directions. I started a historic TV show, served as president of the New York City Trial Lawyers Association, had a renowned and successful legal career, and created a landmark internet company. And through it all I built a multi-million-dollar real estate portfolio that reaches from the seashore in the Hamptons to the slopes of Aspen, Manhattan skyscrapers to a mountaintop farm looking out on endless sky. In every aspect of life, I value diversity. For me, it's not about gaining more assets, it's always about having more creativity.

It's also about inspiring others, personally and professionally. You'll often hear people say they'd like to have the life of somebody who's "made it," who seems to have the money and station to remove all worldly worries. If people don't know enough about someone's overall life and work—perhaps the details, enviable or otherwise, haven't been blasted out across the media landscape, social and otherwise—you'll get comments along the lines of, "I wish I had that guy's job."

Such a statement usually implies that the "job" in question isn't so much of a job at all, but rather a leisurely existence without pressures or cares. Dissuade yourself of any such notion right at this moment. If a job, or a life, looks effortless, chances are it took more work than you can imagine to get there…and to remain there.

So how do you get there?

By telling yourself: I can. I will. I must.

CHAPTER 2

10 ANSWERS TO THE QUESTION… WHY REAL ESTATE?

You can invest in anything. Throughout history, there's been no asset, no idea, that hasn't been able to seduce people to hand over their money to someone else with the hope of making it grow. Treasury bonds or Beanie Babies, rare coins or cryptocurrency, fine art or a fledgling singer's career. Domain names, bull semen, gold Krugerrands, parking spaces: there's a market for everything and people have stocked up on it all. And let's not forget there's the good old stock market. But none of it comes close in scale to the one market where you're going to become an expert investor.

Real estate, quite simply, is the largest financial market in the world. You could add all the stocks, all the bonds, every collateral debt obligation, and it doesn't equal real estate.

Now, investing in real estate, at least the way I do it, plays to particular personality traits. Granted, some of these are innate. Others, however, can be learned.

When I was younger, I would invest in the stock market. When a stock would double, I would sell it, and then it would go up tenfold. And when a stock would go down, I would still have it, gathering dust in the closet. So I knew the stock market wasn't for me. But I've never lost money in real estate. Not one dime.

I've invested millions of dollars in real estate since the 1970s. I've seen mortgage rates in double digits and inflation at nearly 14%. I've seen the housing bubble take prices to unheard of levels and then watched the entire bubble burst at the start of the Great Recession. Olympic boycotts and big bank bailouts, the fall of the Berlin Wall and the birth of the internet. Seven presidents have sat in the Oval Office while I've invested in real estate. Through it all, real estate has made me money.

You want more?

•Real estate is, by its very definition, *real*. You can touch and feel it. It's not some amorphous share of a company in some part of the world you'll never visit, not some enterprise that exists in the cloud without anything truly tangible.

•You can invest in real estate while you have another career. Or more than one other career. Remember, I've been a lawyer, a TV personality, an internet pioneer, a public speaker…and all that time, I was building my real estate portfolio.

When I was a lawyer, I didn't need the income from real

estate, but I invested in real estate over a long-term basis. Things I bought 35 years ago, I still have.

•You can use your real estate to generate income. My partners and I have numerous commercial rentals that have kept cash flowing for decades, all the while appreciating in value—residential properties, retail properties, skyscraper office buildings and land with nothing yet built upon it.

There are so many aspects to real estate: the guy who buys the land, the guy who builds the house. I try to diversify, so when my retail is soft, my residential is good. When they're both down, hopefully my land deals are going well, or the office market is going well.

•Real estate is a strong weapon in battling taxes and inflation. The laws change over time here and there, but taxes, interest, depreciation, maintenance and other financial factors should be taken into account when you're weighing the advantages of investing in real estate.

Real estate, in my opinion, is also a wonderful hedge against inflation. What is inflation but the deterioration of the value of your money? There was a time when, if you took $10 and walked into the grocery store, say, that $10 would buy you four packages of batteries. Inflation goes up, and those batteries cost more money, so that same $10 might buy only three packs of batteries. So you have less buying power.

If you have hard assets like real estate, as inflation goes up, the real estate value goes up, and your rental income goes up. Many commercial real estate contracts even have the rent tied in to the consumer price index, so as inflation goes up, so does your rental income.

With that said, rising interest rates in and of themselves are not good for real estate per se, because that elevates the cost of borrowing and maintaining your property. But with adjustable rate mortgages (ARMs), if interest rates rise, that means the economy is stronger and inflation is rising, so even though I'm paying more money to the bank—because interest rates are going up—my rents are going up and the value of the asset is going up. On the other side, when the economy is bad, my interest rates go down, but the value of my property and my rents, historically, do not fall as much.

•Real estate does not suffer the daily volatility of the stock market, where ups and downs are reported and obsessed over on a minute-by-minute—or faster, now—basis. Do you really want to be investing in antacids because of your stock investments?

It goes back to my belief that I would never do well buying equities. It didn't fit my personality. My personality is to buy and hold for the long term. Stocks need constant watching, constant buying and selling.

I don't know if you've ever tried to sell a stock when the

market is going down, but it's not a pretty affair, especially if it's over-the-counter. I once had a stock, I wanted to get rid of it, so I called my broker and he said, "The market maker isn't buying anymore." I said, "What do you mean, the market maker?" He said, "This is a pink sheet item and there are certain over-the-counter firms that make…." My head was spinning. It simply wasn't for me.

•There's never a bad time to start investing in real estate. When the economy is soaring, it's a fine time to get in. When the economy is sinking, it's a fine time to get in. People always need places to live, office space to house their companies, storefronts from which to run a small business, land on which to build a mansion. Regardless of whether they want to buy or rent, if you own it, these people need what you have. There's a demand for what you can supply.

•You're the master of your own destiny. When you buy stock in a company, you're now at the whim of the company's management, its workers, even its customers. When you create your own real estate deals, you're in charge of everything.

•You can involve family and friends. By the end of this book, you're going to know what it takes to come up with a plan for investing, and then how to choose investors. I started with those closest to me: high school friends and my own kids, and made them all money, time after time.

•Good-location real estate always, in the long term. grows in value. Always. It's that simple. There are no guarantees in life, but that's about as close as you can come. It won't happen overnight (although every now and then…), but over time, it makes you money.

By 2017, 31 of the top 50 metro areas in the United States saw median home sales prices get back above pre–Great Recession levels. Yes, that took almost a decade, but you can also think of it as, Wow, even in the worst financial situation our country has faced since the 1930s, real estate came back. And remember, that number is derived from a range of markets: good and not so good. When you invest in the best locations, that recovery is faster and stronger than anywhere else.

•You don't have to be a genius to invest in real estate. You just have to be patient. It's a slow, reliable, methodical investment vehicle. It's the easiest route to financial security that I have ever seen.

CHAPTER 3

YOU NEVER FORGET YOUR FIRST TIME

You're still reading. Good. But that doesn't mean you've definitively decided that real estate investing is really for you. Perhaps you're convinced that only the wealthy can get into the real estate game and become legitimate players. Or it could be that you think there are faster ways to wealth, more glamorous roads to riches. There's an excellent chance that if you are holding this book right now, you might not actually be interested in real estate at all, but you're simply intrigued by the concept of "I Can, I Will, I Must" and you want to see how it plays out.

For what it's worth: I didn't start out with a dream of building a real estate portfolio. There were no childhood visions of owning homes in areas where the world's rich and famous go to play, no plans hatched in homeroom of building houses in the Hamptons, no grand reckoning while driving a taxi through New York City that I'd one day own buildings right there in the Big Apple, renting apartments and reselling commercial properties where businesses would flourish.

No, there weren't years of early training or inspirational role models in the real estate business. No family members to tutor me or even suggest that real estate was truly a business worth pursuing. When the pivotal moment arrived I was already a lawyer, married, building a practice—but in personal injury, not anything to do with real estate. Yes, I had dreams of bigger things, of creating wealth and a financially strong future for myself and a family that would one day arrive. But that didn't set me apart from, well, millions of others.

What sets anyone apart in that crowded field of financial aspiration is inspiration.

What made the difference for me was a trip to the dentist.

I remember the first time I decided to go into real estate. I was in the dentist's office and *Forbes* magazine was there, with the Forbes 400—the richest people in the United States. The *Forbes* list of those 400 people has captured the imagination of not just the business world and has, since launching in 1982, become part of the pop culture zeitgeist. Names like Buffett and Bloomberg, Walton and Gates have been perennial staples on the list and fodder for dreamers in all walks of life. Billionaires can have that kind of effect. For me, though, it wasn't any one individual among the 400 who flicked the switch on the light bulb. Rather, it was a realization that came after examining the names and the sources of their empires.

They said what they did to actually make their money, whether it was inherited or a business, and I kept seeing real estate, real estate, real estate. I said, "Boy, that must be the place to be. Look at all these Forbes 400s."

(It's okay if you've inherited millions or even billions, you can still keep reading.)

I used to walk across the Brooklyn Bridge, because I lived in Brooklyn and I worked in Manhattan. I remember sitting on the bridge one day, on a bench, looking at Manhattan and saying to myself—and this is when we had debts, I didn't have *assets*, I had just graduated law school and we owed $30,000—*Someday I'm going to own a piece of that island.*

Okay, make that a few pieces. Today my partners and I have an office building and residential apartments, even air rights above a building—yes, that's a thing. You could be walking through South Street Seaport or Tribeca or the U.N. Plaza, and in any of them you'd be in my neighborhood. I've gone far afield from New York City with my investments by this point in time, but that's where it began. Well, sort of. The rising spires of glass and steel of the most famous skyline in the world may have sparked my dream, but when it came time to wade into the investing waters, I went first to the mountains.

It was 1977, and I'd just settled a case. A big one. After nearly five years, the first large fee of my career had arrived, $21,000, and I knew exactly what I wanted to do with it. It wasn't headed for some securities account, it wasn't going into the stock market. Real estate was its destination. It was only a matter of where.

In those days, my wife, Judy, and I would take vacations by hopping in the car and lighting out of the city without any destination in mind. We were heading up the New York State Thruway on one of those journeys when I saw the sign for Route 84. I turned to my wife and said that I'd seen an advertisement for a community called Hemlock Farms, off Route 84.

So, naturally, being young and adventurous, we went west on Route 84 and got off the exit for Hemlock Farms.

We wound up renting a house there for that vacation week, and were instantly drawn to the community. Although we were renting an apartment at the time, and we'd never owned anything, we were looking for a second home instead of a first home. We didn't have to look for long, and found a 1,700-squre-foot, four-bedroom house on a pond with beautiful water views. With an 8 ¾% mortgage, I bought my very first property.

The Poconos was certainly not the best place to invest. But every year we used the house and it would go up in value. And I was able to deduct the taxes and the interest expense on my mortgage. So I felt it was a good investment, because the house was going up in value, I used it and I saw it as a free vacation for myself and my family.

The house was two hours from New York, and Judy and our two kids would spend summers there while I would work back at the law firm in the city and come up for long weekends. A hilly area with plenty of snow in the winter, the Poconos offered a respite from Manhattan and wonderful vacations, but it was not an investment-grade area—although we sold it in 1999 for three times the purchase price.

But we had it for many, many years. Historically there was more supply than demand in the Poconos, and it really wasn't a comparable investment to Manhattan, Brooklyn or the Hamptons. I recognized those three other locations, even Aspen, were more significant from an investment point of view. It's the old saying—location, location location—and you always want to have property where there's more demand than supply.

One year after I bought the Poconos home, I settled another big case. My family was living in a rented duplex in Park Slope, Brooklyn, and a brownstone across the street went up for sale for $120,000. With a $12,000 deposit and the belief that I was in a market where such a buy would improve over the long haul, one where demand would outpace supply, I made my second real estate purchase.

A home for my family.

CHAPTER 4

WELCOME TO THE HAMPTONS

In April 2014, a jolt went through the national real estate news cycle when word came that Copper Beech Farm in Greenwich, Connecticut, had sold for $120 million. Champagne corks popped and toasts were raised in certain circles to its being the most expensive residential property deal in the history of the United States.

Before the bubbles in those glasses even had a chance to go flat, shockwaves emanated from the eastern end of Long Island, New York. Casual fans of the real estate game and industry insiders alike were stunned when, only three weeks after the Copper Beech Farm deal was announced, it was revealed that East Hampton was home to the new champ on the list of priciest residential deals: an 18-acre estate at 60 Further Lane had sold for $147 million.

That record has since been broken, a fate meant for all records. Even without this distinction, the Hamptons is a singular place, though not a single location. Depending on who you ask you'll get differing answers and opinions, but for our purposes let's just say the Hamptons is a collection of towns, villages and hamlets that begins about 77 miles east of New York City in Westhampton and extends all the way to the Montauk Lighthouse, which George

Washington himself commissioned, at the easternmost point of Long Island. Its beach communities, filled with high-end restaurants and shops and polo and art shows, have earned it the moniker of Summer Playground for the Rich and Famous. And those Atlantic Ocean beaches are nothing short of spectacular. Coopers Beach in Southampton and Main Beach in East Hampton have separately been named the Top Beach in the World in an annual survey that ranks such things, and they might not even be the best of the bunch along this southern shore of Long Island.

But sand and surf are only part of the allure. All this is not a recent development, either. There is a wondrous natural light in the Hamptons, a glow that attracted artists such as Jackson Pollock and Lee Krasner and Willem de Kooning decades before anybody thought this place would become the setting of America's priciest home. The power elite from Wall Street and Hollywood alike are drawn here for what they see as a bucolic, rural wonderland that echoes a small-town America many fear lost, courtesy of farmers and fishermen with family names going back centuries. Sagaponack, which lies just east of Bridgehampton, has been rated the most expensive zip code in America more than once, most recently in 2016, when the median home value in 11962 was $5.5 million. That's a long way to come for land that once held nothing but acres and acres of potato fields south of the highway.

That highway is Montauk Highway, and to be south of it in Hamptons real estate parlance is to be in the most exclusive of environs. Typically, the farther south of that highway you go, the farther north the prices will climb.

To give the uninitiated some perspective, not every Hamptons home sale reaches such nosebleed-inducing heights as the record setter on Further Lane. As of the summer of 2018, the median home price in the Hamptons hovered around $1 million, give or take. The "middle" range starts around $5 million. At the "high end" you're talking $10 million and up.

And it's not only a seasonal locale. There is a community that lives in the Hamptons year-round, the working class and middle class and professionals who make up many other small towns across the country. But there's no denying the fact that the real estate here is special, and it draws a certain crowd. Walk down the streets, grab a table at a local eatery—especially in summer—and there's a decent chance you'll find yourself there with Billy Joel and Alec Baldwin, Madonna and Steven Spielberg, Gwyneth Paltrow and Jimmy Fallon, Martha Stewart and Eli Manning, Jennifer Lopez and Jimmy Buffett, Ralph Lauren and Robert DeNiro, Ron Perelman and Michael Bloomberg, the Koch Brothers and Ira Rennert…well, you get the picture.

Jackie Bouvier grew up riding horses at her family home in

East Hampton, the same town where Marilyn Monroe and Arthur Miller had a summer cottage in their happier days, the same town where Jerry Seinfeld currently has a home that sports, among other accoutrements, its own baseball field. Incredible as it may seem, a personal ball field is not such a big deal in the Hamptons. Heads rarely turn for such amenities as rooftop tennis courts, basements with bowling alleys and halfpipes, even professional croquet fields. (Don't feel bad if this the first time you've heard that there's such a thing as professional croquet.) Pool houses have their own gourmet kitchens and workout rooms, saunas and game rooms, some of them soaring three stories high.

The real estate is so famous, it has starred in such movies as *Eternal Sunshine of the Spotless Mind* (the house is named Kilkare, in case you're playing Trivial Pursuit) and *Something's Gotta Give* (Diane Keaton's digs sold for $41 million in 2014, some 11 years after the film was shot), *Grey Gardens* (you know a house is important when it lends its name to a film about Jackie Kennedy's cousins) and *Pollock* (yes, that's really Jackson Pollock's home onscreen). TV shows like ABC's *Revenge* and Showtime's *Billions* have used over-the-top homes to embody the wealth and power inherent in this place.

To arrive in this land of luxury by car—which, despite the helicopters and planes that create an omnipresent overhead buzz in summertime, remains the most popular means of transportation—driving east from Manhattan, just about 90 miles out, you cross the Shinnecock Canal. The waterway was dug out in 1892, connecting the Atlantic Ocean and Shinnecock Bay to Great Peconic Bay and the North Fork of Long Island. This north-south link is not as important as the east-west line of demarcation the canal cuts between what many call the "Real Hamptons" and, well, everywhere else.

Keep the pedal down for a few minutes after crossing that Rubicon into Southampton Village and look to your right (that's south as you enter this land of billionaires and Bonackers—the historic name given to the blue-collar residents of the Springs area of East Hampton, derived from Accabonac Harbor). You'll see a property sitting unassumingly sentry-like up on a small rise of land just above a gas station.

This is the first hotel you'll see in the Hamptons.

It is mine.

If you haven't been to the Hamptons, you may be imagining a sprawling resort, ocean views and infinity pools, five-star dining and organic seaweed wrap spa treatments. Such a spot will have to remain there in your mind. The hotel, built in 1970, is a modest affair...but wait, we're getting ahead of ourselves here. This is about my first foray into Hamptons real estate, not my most recent. More about that later.

I first came out to the Hamptons in 1986, drawn by an ad for a home on the back of *The New York Times Magazine*. My wife and I were looking at another investment, a house in Connecticut, and then I see this ad—$425,000, pool, tennis and ocean view. So we took a ride out to meet with the broker.

At the time I knew nothing about the Hamptons, absolutely nothing. I'd been out to the Hamptons maybe once before. When I was 18, I went out to Southampton with a friend, and I remember seeing all these incredible houses, all this incredible land, seeing all these long driveways—it was like nothing I'd ever seen.

Bridgehampton is the home to auto racing in America and to baseball Hall of Famer Carl Yastrzemski. The famous steakhouse Bobby Van's originated here. There's even a legend that the Stars and Stripes was created by Bridgehampton resident John Hulbert back during the Revolutionary War. It's as good a place as any to set an origin story.

I saw the house, and I said, "I see the pool, I see the tennis, it's a very nice contemporary home, but where's the ocean view?" The broker takes me to the upstairs terrace and says, "You see that blue over there?" I said, "That blue over there? That's 2 miles away!" He said, "Well, that's the ocean."

Anyway, I liked it and I gave him a good-faith check. That was in Bridgehampton, south of the highway. I had no idea where Bridgehampton was, I had no idea what south of the highway was, but I was smitten.

Then I went around the area with another broker, who showed me everything that was in my price range. I learned what south of the highway was, what north of the highway meant, that being able to get directly to the beach was a good thing. And I learned that there was nothing better than that first house—especially when the first broker told me about renting the property out for the summer. Starting right away.

I paid $415,000 for the home, and immediately rented if for $50,000 that first summer. I remember, the tenant moved in and said there was not enough furniture, no rugs, no art on the wall. So Judy and my nephew and I rented a truck, and we actually took the paintings off the wall in my house in Brooklyn and the rugs off the floor, and I moved them out to the Hamptons.

I continued to rent that house every year, until I sold it for $3.1 million in 2006. In 1998, I bought a second Bridgehampton home, a stone house not unlike a Tuscan villa, for $2.2 million. This time I bought a good deal of the owner's furniture as well, and I've rented that to the same tenant since 2005.

Nearly 20 years after I purchased that initial home, I dramatically increased my footprint in the Hamptons real estate market. There was a 26-acre development in Bridgehampton, which I purchased for $12 million in 2005 with a group of family and friends, and which we sold for $37.5 million in 2007. Our group also purchased 42 acres of Sagaponack farmland for $25 million that became the famous Sagaponack Greens, one of the most notable Hamptons deals of the new millennium, especially when we sold off eight lots in the most challenging real estate recession I've ever experienced.

But we're getting ahead of ourselves here. First things first...

CHAPTER 5

HOW TO FIND YOUR MARKET

The best place to start is at the beginning. And so far, you've done that. You've picked up this book. Good start, indeed. You've thought about it and concluded that learning about real estate investing is for you. Or at least that it might be for you, and you're willing to go on a few more pages. You understand that this is a slow-growth proposition, not a get-wealthy-overnight deal—or you're at least not rejecting the notion outright and are willing to be convinced at some point. Maybe you just love my positive attitude and want to hear more. Or you want to go to the Hamptons. In any case, you want to take the next step.

So now what?

Naturally, more and more questions begin to arise. I've said that timing doesn't matter, but place most certainly does. "Location, location, location" are the three magic words. But it's a big world out there. *So where do I begin looking for that ideal investment property? Is that I'm-going-to-be-searching-for-a-needle-in-a-haystack sort of feeling in my gut normal? I am ready for the process to begin in earnest, but how do I know where to start?*

I always start in the same place. It is exactly where you're going to begin. But that place isn't at the top. It isn't steps from the finish line. Like a Super Bowl quarterback who begins by throwing a beat-up old ball around his backyard years before tossing touchdowns in the big game, the early phases of any success story are steeped in preparation and hard work. You can become a real-estate superstar—keep believing that—but you can't become one overnight.

First, you have to do your due diligence. You have to do your homework. You have to do the 95% perspiration before you get to the 5% inspiration. First you have to pick a particular area and learn real estate—you have to *teach* yourself real estate. You're not going to learn it exclusively from me.

Hold on a minute. Didn't you pick up this book to learn about real estate from one of the masters? Yes, you did. That fact hasn't changed. Now you're going to start learning *how to learn.*

You're going to learn real estate through your own hard work and due diligence. I can show you how to do it, but I can't teach you what properties to buy. Only you can do that. And first you have to understand a market.

Any fool can *know*, Albert Einstein noted, but the point is to *understand.* To understand a market, you have to immerse yourself in it. It matters not where said market is, mind you. You can begin by picking a market where you live, right outside your front door, where you shop and dine and are intimate with many aspects of life. Or you can choose a market that has long intrigued you but that is, as you begin, a mystery.

In any case, you're going to get inside every corner and cranny, turn it inside out, and know it better than you could possibly imagine. Don't worry, you're not going to do it alone. There are resources at your disposal, and I've spent years honing the approach for making those resources work for me. And now, for you.

Finding the best real estate location is just like the circular rings when you throw a pebble in a pond. The best location is where the rock hits the water. As the rings spread in greater and greater distance from the center, the less valuable the property is. The best locations go up first and go up most in a rising market, and in a declining market they go down least and go down last. Conversely, the opposite is true for marginal locations.

You may not be able to afford premium locations in the beginning. At first I could only afford what I considered "bridge areas." I couldn't afford to buy in premium zip codes, but I figured out that I would try to buy something between two good areas—I was young and I had time—until both areas expanded. And it worked out very well. Some of those properties I still have.

An excellent place to start is where all of us unearth endless reams of information from the silly to the sublime. Go on the internet—a wonderful place to learn about real estate markets.

Zillow, MLS, Redfin, StreetEasy—in the next chapter, you'll read more about the portals, how to use them, how to tread carefully as you walk yourself through sprawling forests of data. For the moment, it's enough to know that the information you'll find there isn't going to end your search; it's going to start and inform it. These sites aren't going to replace real estate brokers in your world. In fact, the internet can actually help you optimize the relationship with your brokers.

Online research is no substitute for a broker. (You'll see why in the "Love, Love Me Due Diligence" chapter.) Rather, I use it to make myself knowledgeable about how to speak to a broker. The internet, in other words, evens the playing field. Years ago, you had to go around with three brokers, and each one would tell you something different. Through the internet, you can gain a lot of information to start the conversation.

So, back to that question that began this chapter. Where to begin?

Small. Local. Targeted. It doesn't matter if you're in a rural, suburban or urban marketplace. Take one area, or a 10-square-block area, or one particular town, and learn it.

Know every house on the market, or every commercial building, whatever you're looking for. Take notes. Find out what buildings or houses are listed for, along with what they've historically sold for in that particular neighborhood. Know all the prices. Know all the details. Then go around with a number of brokers and see them all.

It's a sentiment that bears repeating. There is *no substitute* for physically seeing the properties you read about online, going there and getting a first-hand experience. The sights, the smells, the surroundings—these are as important as the numbers themselves.

Don't just say, *"Oh, it sold for so much and so much on Ashley Place."* Look at it, feel it.

And do that as often as you need to in order to fully absorb it, to understand it.

You walk around. You look at the outside of a place, the inside. You say to yourself, "Oh, this sold for $750,000 on this block," and you have an idea of what's involved at that asking price. And then when you see another project, and a broker takes you around or you see it on the internet, you'll be able to say, "Boy, that's a good deal, because I've seen four other projects for $200,000 more than this one, and all I have to do is a little work."

You might start out here thinking that every property you

look at should be pristine. This is as good a moment as any to let you know that it may become perfectly normal if you start to smile when you walk in to see a property on your list and it's run-down. That's a great way to find a value buy! Not *falling* down, but a bit run down. It can be dirty and seem unloved. The paint can be old and cracking, wallpaper peeling and curling off the wall like it's the set of a *Barton Fink* remake. If there's cat hair all over the furniture, *fantastic*, you'll think. If the kitchen hasn't been updated since the Eisenhower administration, *awesome*, you'll say.

In many cases, these issues can give you negotiating leverage to bring an asking price down—or, because of their effect on the seller in pricing the property, the asking price may be lower than otherwise comparable properties to begin with—and you can get the house at a price that is advantageous to you. All it'll take is some updates and upgrades, a little work on your part to make necessary improvements and bring it to a level that suits your vision.

Personally, I love doing the work, because as soon as I do it, I've added value to the project. When I can get a value buy, I want a value buy I can fix up. Why is that? When you see something that needs work, fewer people want to buy it—they don't have the capacity or the vision or they're too busy to fix it up. And when you fix up something like that, it immediately increases in value. (Of course, you must remember that unless you do the work yourself, you need to have dependable, skilled tradespeople who will do quality work at a fair price.)

There are two ways real estate appreciates: One, the market increases in that particular location or area. Two, you add value through improvement.

What's great about fixing up a property a little bit and coming in on a value buy is that you're immediately ahead of the game. Whether it's the interior or exterior, all improvements add value. That being said, the best things to add to a property are new kitchens and baths. If you put in a new finished basement, it doesn't typically add as much value as kitchens and baths. In some sense, though, it depends on what your buyers are looking for.

The whole "improvements" notion may not be in your wheelhouse, nor in your plans. That's fine right now. You're putting in all the effort of researching prices and other details. You're becoming a bona fide expert in every aspect of your chosen area. You'll come to know asking prices, yes, but you'll also know what amenities come with those prices. You'll know that one block always sells quickly, while another has homes that sit on the market for what seems like an eternity. You'll know what people are paying in rent, in taxes. You'll know how close you are to public transportation and shopping, you'll know the quality of the school district. You'll know it all. And you need to know right now that gaining this knowledge is the very definition of hard work.

You have to do your homework, and once you've done that, you've learned the area, you know the prices, you know the demand for the area at certain price points, you know the market, then you know when a value buy comes up.

For example, you know that the market you are researching goes up 6% or 7% a year, or you know that you can get $2,000 a month for that apartment, and you know you can get $6,000 rent for that store because you've seen it. You've been working this project now for six months, so you know what you can do, you know what you can get.

Looking at the current state of a market will only get you halfway to your goal, however. In the world of real estate research, you're going to find that past is often prologue. Let me explain.

From an objective point of view, the best approach you can take is to do a study over the last 10, 15, 20 years, of the appreciation of that particular area. And all those numbers are available to anyone. This is so much easier today than when my real estate journey began. Today, of course, we have the internet, where the information is mere keystrokes away, and you can find historical data for almost any given property.

And if you find that the area you are researching goes up 8% a year, over a 20-year period or more, you know that's a good project, and that's unlikely to be changed. Good areas only get better. So when a market is down, you know because you've done your homework. You've done your due diligence. When a market rises 8% over 20 years—and there have been many down markets in those 20 years—history shows that the trend is going to continue like that. *History* shows it. Time reveals it. Remember, this is an investment for the long haul, not a get-rich-quick approach.

This type of analysis has served me well no matter what part of the country I've investigated. I've done it in the Hamptons, in Brooklyn, by the ocean and at higher altitudes.

Location. Area. These attributes outweigh the physical aspects of a house or a building itself. There's a time and place to discuss architectural style. We can debate the relative value of a pool, an elevator or a wine cellar. We can discuss the merits of top-tier appliances or smart-home sophistications. But it all goes back to knowing where to start, and where to keep your focus.

Location. Area.

One of the basic facts I've learned over decades of real estate investing is that what goes up is the value of the land. I believe land is the most important segment of property appreciation. Never buy the improvement—buy the land. The improvements normally don't increase in value. Why? Because I can always rebuild the house—unless it's such an unusual house, one that could only be built at that price at that time when they first built it, but that's unusual. In most cases, it's the land that appreciates, and the house goes with it.

This probably has you thinking, *Okay, so do I want to buy a house or building for resale, or do I want to buy land and build on it?* There's no universal answer to this question. You'll arrive at the answer by asking yourself other questions during your research. Building a house is a massive undertaking. Do you have the patience and propensity for taking on large projects? Do you have a head for details? Your answers will guide you, as will your acquired knowledge of the value and potential of land and development within your chosen area.

A key question is, what will it cost to build that house? There are a multitude of calculations and considerations. You have to factor in today's building cost, today's labor cost, professional fees and the time and effort you will expend to make all the decisions that go into building a house. Don't forget the year or longer it's going to take for you to move into the house. Those are usually the determining factors if you want to buy a resale or build on land.

Normally you get a better value when you build. It's generally less expensive in the long run, but it takes time and effort, and many people don't want to invest that time and energy. You may want to, you may not. Either is fine.

You can do anything you want. That's what *I Can, I Will, I Must* is all about, as a book and as a philosophy. Keep that in mind as you go on.

Okay, now it's time to go start diving into that market of yours, wherever it may be.

CHAPTER 6

LOVE, LOVE ME DUE DILIGENCE

It doesn't matter if we're talking about cars, dishwashers, plumbers, Pusheen pillows, sneakers, smartphones or anything else. It comes down to a single, immutable fact:

Every purchase we make starts with an online search.

Depending on who you ask, anywhere from 80% to 97% of all purchases start with somebody typing something into a search engine. And why not? Searching before buying makes perfect sense. It makes us all more informed consumers. We compare prices, quality, availability, you name it. And not just for consumer goods. You knew we were coming to this… the internet is dominant in real estate.

More than 75% of all real estate findings and leads originate with the internet. By that I mean people searching on sites like Zillow, Trulia and Redfin. These sites allow you to view any kind of real estate that strikes your fancy. There are also scores of Multiple Listing Services (MLS), Realtor.com, and several For Sale By Owner sites (FSBO). You'll come across a variety of databases and resources on your journey.

If commercial real estate is your area of choice,

Loopnet.com and Crexi.com are the major players (that is as of the moment this sentence is being written—something new may be launched tomorrow!), dealing with everything from multifamily properties to shopping centers.

On almost any of the above sites, you can search a town, a zip code, even an individual block. You can see what's for sale, for how much, get exact addresses, see photos from inside and out, view aerial maps and more. You can do this over your morning coffee, all through a typical workday (don't tell your boss I said it's okay), or even at 3 a.m. if you wish. This is where, in almost every case, you'll start your serious research into a market.

It is not, however, where that search is going to end. Far from it.

Now, keep in mind, you just use these various websites as a guide to find investment properties or houses that you want to investigate further. They're excellent as far as that is concerned. No longer does one need five brokers to see what's available in a particular area. You go to two or three sites, then evaluate the comparisons from the due diligence every buyer must do, whether it's commercial or residential, to determine whether or not it's for you at the given price. That's how you should use the internet—for the informational start of your search.

As you proceed along your journey, no matter what venture

you undertake, information will be your most valuable asset. The more you know, the further you can go. In real estate, you'll start with researching towns and properties and learning a market, but the time will come when you'll call a broker, then soon you'll be dealing with a lawyer, an engineer, an architect, a land surveyor—all of them coming together for your deal. You're going to rely on these people for their areas of expertise, but you'll get so much more out of the relationships if you've done your research and develop an understanding of the role each plays, of the choices they need to make.

It's all about knowledge. If you want to be successful, even though you're hiring professionals, always be proactive. I need to find the right questions to ask, the issues that I truly need to be concerned with. It's wise to rely on professionals, but it's also beneficial to acquire as much information as possible, so you can be an informed participant. You are going to be asking questions, and information allows you to make sure those questions are the correct one. When I put my money down on the table, I want to know that I am part of the decision-making process: that I know exactly why decisions are being made.

Before decision time arrives, before you're hiring those pros, that information must be gleaned. This might seem daunting. The problem with pages and pages of search results and seemingly infinite data points can be that they are, well, endless. As you're perusing StreetEasy or clicking and scrolling through Zillow, you're going to come upon hundreds of listings. How will you determine which ones are worth your time and which ones you can zip right past?

You're going to set goals, that's how. You are, eventually, going to know exactly what you want to achieve with a particular investment, and that's going to drive your search. Do not be intimidated.

You're only going to stop at a listing that fits your criteria and your goals. The key element when you're searching is to take a piece of paper and write down your goals. It may be price appreciation. It may be a first home now that you're raising a family and you need a good school system. It may be investment only. It may be income. It may be you want a second home in the Hamptons, you want a little status, because all your peers in your industry are out there and you want to make a statement—there's nothing wrong with that.

There's nothing wrong with any of your goals, but you have to understand what they are, and you don't want to deviate. You want to be happy and make a smart investment. That's why I always have my goals in front of me.

First and foremost, real estate is a financial transaction. However, it is also highly emotional. You may walk into a house and love every inch of it. You may want to pay the asking price and move in, but that is an emotional decision. It may not fit your goals. Sometimes it may not be an investment vehicle because it's in an area that's less desirable—it's far from the ocean and takes a half hour to get to the water, for example. The smart move may be a smaller house that's near the water that will appreciate more, and more quickly.

It's fine not to know what your goals are right now. They will become more apparent, and then crystal clear, as you do your research, learn your market and learn about yourself as a potential investor. We aren't there yet. Right now, you are still in the learning-to-learn phase.

A few other questions to answer and things to keep in mind as you work your way through the World Wide Web...

What Is a Multiple Listing Service?

A Multiple Listing Service (MLS) is a site populated by all the licensed real estate brokers and agents in a particular geographical area—there are roughly 700 regional MLS databases around the United States—who pay for the right to be affiliated with a particular site and list homes there. Unless you're a licensed professional, you can't list a property on an MLS, but as a diligent researcher of markets and a prospective buyer, the MLS is an invaluable tool for searching listings and gathering data.

The idea of the MLS actually started all the way back in the 1800s, the National Association of Realtors tells us, when agents got together to network and share information about their respective properties. The hope was that by sharing information, along with compensation on any shared sales, they could help one another move inventory. Over time, the databases moved from files and books to online, where the public can now also view them.

There's something to drop at your next cocktail party.

Data Points by the Zillions

It would be impossible, impractical and a few steps toward the inane for this chapter, or even a whole book, to go through every nuance of every site you may come across. Knowing that you'll most likely be using Zillow, we're going to go with that for most of the examples to follow, knowing that the underlying philosophies for how to use the information you'll discover can be applied to almost any other site.

There is an incredible amount of data Zillow can give you about a property. Zillions of data points, even. Combine that concept of zillions with the notion that a home is not just an instrument of finance, but a place you lay your head—on a pillow—and now you don't need to ask where the name "Zillow" came from. Another one for the cocktail party.

Okay, where were we? Oh, yes, all that data you're going to come across. First, there's the price the seller is asking, right beneath the gallery of photos. You'll also find the number of bedrooms and baths, the square footage and the year built. There are details on appliances, notes on what types of heating and cooling the house has, the number of parking spaces, the lot size, facts about the local schools, and a mortgage calculator.

It may not be every bit of information you want, but it's great place to start, especially since all the information is available, in the same place, for the full range of properties you're researching. It is all up-to-date, and it is also a window to the past.

Know Your History

I love being able to access all this information, and so easily. I believe in knowing not just a property's present but also it past—and an area's past, overall—as a means of evaluating its future. One particularly valuable tool is the Price/Tax History, where you can see every sale price and every annual tax amount ever associated with a house.

I want to know the price history of the particular project or house. That's very, very important. I want to see if it's going down, if it's going up, I want to see what the seller paid for the project. If he paid $2 million for the project two years ago and today he's asking $6 million, I ask myself, well, has the market gone up threefold in two years? I don't think so. Have improvements been added, has the square footage tripled? Or did the seller get a fabulous buy two years ago, something unheard of? Maybe. You ask the listing broker, what has happened with this project that has tripled the price in two years? And if you don't get an answer that satisfies you, you need to do more research to get a satisfactory answer.

Estimates and Zestimates

When you go to view a particular property on Zillow, right below the photos you'll see the listing price, and just below that, in smaller type, you'll see something called a Zestimate. This number is the price that Zillow, through its statistical evaluation, estimates the home could be worth. Handle this number with care.

There are people who look at this number as gospel. If it's higher than the asking price, they'll assume they are getting a great deal. If it's lower than the listing price, they think there is no way they should pay what the seller is asking. Neither of these conclusions is the way you want to approach a Zestimate.

All real estate is local, and all properties are even more local. For a database site to tell you what a property is worth, it really is pushing the boundaries of knowledge. Because what they're doing is telling you what they think the house is worth simply from a statistical point of view.

In all likelihood, somebody from that database has never seen the house, never seen the location, never entered the house, hasn't seen the bathrooms, the kitchens. Thus, you should be careful about putting too much credence on certain valuations. Real estate is so local, so subjective—it's a property's school district, how close it is to public transportation, its proximity to the ocean, to a ski slope, for example, all of which may not be fully evaluated from a statistical-data point of view.

Remember, in real estate something is only worth what someone is willing to pay for it at any given time.

How Many Days on Market Is Too Many Days?

This is another very important stat Zillow will supply, but be careful with this one, too. It is how many days a property has been on the market. Overall, it is useful as a guide toward understanding pricing in a market, but it may not always be what it seems.

When you see a house that's been listed on Zillow for a long time, it in all likelihood means that the house is priced above market value. Trust me, if a house is priced correctly, it will sell. So if it's above market, it means it's so high that they're only getting bids at market but they don't want to sell it.

What does that tell you? How many times have you heard someone say, "This is my number and I'll only sell it at that number!" Well, Mr. Seller, then your house will sit there for 443 days.

Or more.

But be careful of a trick. A house can be taken off the market by a broker and then put back on 30 days later. Well, that starts the days-on-market stat running again, from zero.

Of course, there's no set formula for how long a house can or should stay on the market, although there are experts who can give you a good idea. The appraisal from the bank will have in it an estimate of how long the bank believes it should take a house to sell, and that bank appraiser will know the market well enough to make a fairly accurate assessment.

There really is no hard-and-fast rule, but if a property has been languishing for six or eight months, there are probably issues. If you price a house over market and it sits there all that time, it gets stale. And in the end—I have seen it many, many times—you wind up taking less money than if you'd priced it properly in the beginning. You would likely have sold it in short order and moved on with your life.

Journey back with me for a moment to the Village of East Hampton, one of the most exclusive enclaves in the country. There is a gourmet food shop that is the centerpiece of a building with apartments and additional retail spaces. My partners and I had been eyeing since it went on the market. It was the largest multiple dwelling in the Village, and very well known. The seller was originally asking something like $13 million, an aggressive price.

So I was patient. It sat on the market for five years. The price fell and fell.

I recall it was down to $7 million or $8 million and we offered him $5 million, and they wanted to get out—and the seller gave us back a mortgage for seven years, interest only at 3%. There was nobody making offers to him at that time, we gave him a reasonable offer, and that was it. That's a perfect example of how, if you ask an inflated price for real estate, in the end you take substantially less than if you'd asked a reasonable price in the beginning.

And that is an error that many, many sellers make. They don't understand that the market is very efficient, especially in the Hamptons, in New York City, in many urban areas. If you overprice a property, the odds are you're not going to sell it. You may sell it to that one person who, for some reason, falls in love with the location, who falls in love with the kitchen, who falls in love with the bathroom, who falls in love with you for whatever reason. But you know what?

That's a story that happens to some other fortunate seller—it never happens to you.

Some people might call that East Hampton Village deal a lucky break. And I won't argue about the role fate sometimes plays with fortune. Luck does have a lot to do with it. But you also create your own luck by being patient.

CHAPTER 7

BE CONTENT TO GROW RICH SLOWLY

I Can, I Will, I Must is about to become a multisensory experience, if you're up to the challenge. At this point, it is recommended you take whatever device you find preferable and put on the theme music to *Chariots of Fire* or *Rocky*, or both, on loop, if you are so inclined. If we could have included such a soundtrack with this chapter, we would have. Maybe in a future edition.

In the early 1980s, I suffered a debilitating back injury, the kind that would have kept many people down for the count. I was out of work for two months after surgery. As part of the rehabilitation, I began walking. It went slowly at first, and was excruciating at times. Over months, my physical condition improved, and I covered more and more ground. Eventually, that evolved into running.

The goal wasn't really to get anywhere more quickly, but to push myself a little harder, to get a little farther each time. Every day, a little farther still. It started with one mile, then a few more, until...

26.2.

When I lived in Park Slope, Brooklyn, the New York City Marathon went right through 4th Avenue in my neighborhood, and I used to go down and watch the runners pass through on those brisk early autumn days on their way to the big finish in the big city. I wasn't a runner at the time—I didn't even walk long distances yet—but I found inspiration in those feet pounding the asphalt, some at a world-record pace, others setting down a slower but no less determined rhythm.

I said to myself, You know what, I can run a marathon. I can do this.

So I started walking. Before I ran, I walked. I walked a little bit, then a little longer, then a little longer, and I trained myself to walk long distances. Then I started running slowly. I would run a little bit, then a little more, then a little more.

Prospect Park in Brooklyn was designed by Frederick Law Omsted and Calvert Vaux, the same men who created Manhattan's Central Park, its 526 acres originally designed both for the masses to enjoy its open space and for the wealthy to develop the surrounding real estate. I began running there, and eventually met a small group of like-minded men, in varying degrees of physical shape but all with the same sense of dedication.

The cadre would meet each and every day, and we were going to run. This was the Just Do It mentality before anyone had put that term on a T-shirt. We'd meet in the morning at seven to jog around the park, and in time our vision crystalized. Mind you, not one of us had ever run a marathon before, but we decided that we'd sign up and embrace the challenge.

Simply considering the idea of a marathon can be daunting. There's a very real reason that people use the term *marathon* itself to describe long, arduous, seemingly endless rigors in all walks of life. It's not easily conquered, and certainly not overnight nor on a whim. You must go the distance. You must prepare, and you cannot take a shortcut. You cannot see the finish line when you begin, yet you must know you're going to get there.

The whole idea was to break through a wall of unknowns, of "I can't do it," of "It's impossible for me to do it," and to say, *Yes I Can*. And of course, I had my quotes. *I can, I will, I must. I can, I will, I must.* I kept saying that to myself. *Attitude equals altitude. Nothing can be done without hope and confidence.* If I say it, I can believe it.

Allow the camera to pan in on me, slow motion, running through Prospect Park, beneath the canopy of trees and on the open road. Cut away to me ascending the hills of Pennsylvania's Pocono Mountains, pushing through a training regimen, sometimes running up to 24 miles a day. Rain, shine, the odometer keeps clicking.

Of the 15 marathons I ran, the first was the one I was best

trained for. By the way, the 15th marathon is just as hard as the first marathon. I couldn't figure it out. You think it would get easier, but it never got easier. It never got easier!

The New York City Marathon is the largest in the world, with more than 50,000 runners gathering to traverse its famed five boroughs, through Staten Island, Brooklyn, Queens, the Bronx and finally Manhattan itself. Crowds of thousands line the streets throughout the entire course, cheering on friends, family, strangers, anyone bold enough to have laced up the sneakers and pinned a number to their chest. I still recall being there at the start, ready to take that first step on a journey of not 1,000 miles, but one that sure might feel like it. Fear wasn't the emotion coursing through me, not apprehension, not even second thoughts, which are all feelings any number of marathoners will admit to, even if they've run in Pheidippides' footsteps before.

We were standing in Staten Island, and I knew I was going to complete 26.2 miles, if I had to crawl my last mile on my hands and knees, digging my nails into the ground. I was going to finish, whatever I had to do.

It's a philosophy I've applied to each of my marathons, literal and figurative. I admit, the first one remains special. It proves something different than the others do. Yet every long journey is memorable, an achievement to be celebrated, and not always so much for reaching the finish line.

It's setting a goal and then achieving it. But it's not the achievement alone—it's the work to achieve the goal. And so every time before I finish and achieve my goal, I've already set a new goal, because I know I'm on my way and I'm going to achieve it. The road to the goal, the work, the achievement, the training, that's really the wonderful part to me.

I never passed by Baruch College on Lexington Avenue during any of those marathons, but my morning walks through the Big Apple have led me past its buildings and halls many times. The school's namesake—legendary self-made investor and businessman, advisor to Woodrow Wilson and FDR—was not a marathoner, as far as we know, but he certainly understood a marathoner's mindset.

Bernard Baruch, one of the greatest financiers of the 19th century, used to sit on a park bench and give advice. And one of his pieces of advice was, "If you're not content to grow rich slowly, you probably won't."

That sound you are about to hear is the collective wind being sucked out of every hotel conference room and convention center hosting every get-rich-quick seminar in the country at this very moment.

If you've never been to one of these things yourself, you're probably at least familiar with the notion. Slick, sharply dressed hosts up on stage with a headset, promises of quick, easy wealth, buffet lunch in some hotel ballroom, maybe a set of take-home books or downloadable course materials. One day, or a weekend at most, and you're going to be an expert, ready to start making money and calling your own shots.

I've been to these seminars—not as a participant, not as a student, but as an observer. Some people go see *Hamilton* on a Saturday afternoon (if you are one of them, good for you—at least you know what you're getting back for your investment). I've spent many hours sitting in a sea of dreamers and fast-talking lecturers tossing out platitudes and promises of wealth. It's a chance to learn—not what these self-proclaimed experts are teaching, but what the audience is buying into, how human nature works. It's also a chance to confirm that the only one guaranteed to grow his money quickly in that room is the guy whose name is on the marquee out front.

Of course, these conferences are not the only places where dreams of fast bucks are flying. We read about them every day, see the talking heads on TV raving about super bargain prices on stocks that are a *sure thing to go up* if you just *get in now*, about the day trader who turned $1,000 into a small fortune by swapping stocks like they were chips at the craps table, fast and furious. Don't be shocked when you meet someone who watched a stock triple in value in a week's trading time who's now convinced that all he needs is a little guidance and maybe a few take-home courses to become Warren Buffett in a month.

The world of real estate has increasingly been drawn into this fast-money mentality, particularly with the wealth of TV shows starring flippers and speculators turning around projects and turning massive profits in 30-minute increments. They're beautiful and funny and sassy and sensational, they make it seem Oh So Easy, and they are sending the same message: Why wait? It's real estate, it's easy! It's all here for the taking right now!

It doesn't matter if these people are buying and selling and making overnight profits in California or the Caribbean, Texas or Timbuktu. There are plenty of people with the same "I Want an Oompa Loompa now!" mentality.

I've been in the business 40 years, and I've never seen what these TV people say happens continue on an ongoing basis. It may happen to one person, to that guy on TV maybe, but you have to look at what happens generally. Flipping may work for some people when the market is robust and rising fast, but trust me, no market moves in one direction. The trend is up on a long-term basis, but you have to have a long-term view. It's the same with the stock market. People are buying when the market is going up, up, up—everything they buy is going up, up, up—but eventually they're going to get caught, because there's no more buying.

Decades ago, I read an article about the revitalization of Atlantic Avenue and Flatbush Avenue in Brooklyn, an area where today you'll find the Barclays Center, home to the NBA's Brooklyn Nets and the site of sold-out events from March Madness to concerts by everyone who's anyone, Billy Joel to Jay-Z. This was light years before the now world-famous arena went up in 2012, when the area was, shall we say, challenged. But there was a silver lining to the cloud that had settled over this spot, one that presented a golden opportunity.

It was a great location, with a huge amount of traffic, courtesy of several major public transportation hubs right there. With the promise of revitalization, with both public and private dollars on the way, with its proximity to Manhattan, this was a location I knew would blossom. So my partners and I started investing in buildings all around, on Fourth Avenue, on Washington Street, on Vanderbilt Street, on Fulton Street.

They were mostly mixed-use buildings that generated profit from the start. We reaped the rewards that solid, income-generating properties offer, but it took more than two decades to see the area's long-promised revitalization actually become a reality. Amid the many stops and starts in the neighborhood's rebirth, I could have decided the wait would go on forever, and sold. Nobody would have questioned the move. Instead, we kept all the buildings except one. Today, there are no mortgages on them, and they've gone up tremendously. It took me 25 years to become an overnight success!

Those who are not content to grow rich slowly probably won't.

I actually put those words on the wall in my first apartment, in Manhattan on 75th Street, when I first entered law school. And I remember exactly where it was when I read the quote.

I was sitting on a park bench, and I was reading an article about Baruch's pearls of wisdom. When I read that, it hit me that that was how I wanted to do it. Here was a financier who actually had a school named after him, and I said, Boy, I want to take a lesson from an experienced person that truly works. There's no substitute for experience.

Money was always an issue in my family growing up, and this quote told me that attaining wealth was not going to happen overnight, that patience was important. That phrase is meaningful to me, and it really set my life. I became very patient early on to invest for the long term, never invest for the quick dollar.

But just because I was content to build success over time doesn't mean that I wasn't planning for it all along. Even as a kid growing up in post-war Brooklyn, well before I hung

Baruch's words on the wall or crossed a marathon finish line, I was taking experiences and building one upon another, each a step toward a goal.

I always wanted to be successful, it wasn't something that came as an afterthought. Every experience, large and small, has been a factor in my growth.

Not all were a walk in the park.

CHAPTER 8

RISK & REWARD

The unconscious body on the floor stares back at me, only a few feet away. Its eyes are open, but there is uncertainty as to the life behind them.

I'm hiding under the kitchen table, seeking refuge from the horror unfolding in the hearth of my home. My father has given my mother another beating, and now here he is, lying motionless save for his shallow breathing.

Such scenes played out often in the early years of my life. One of my earliest memories is this one, when my mother was defending herself and hit my father over the head with a frying pan. She would protect herself with pots and pans, whatever was available. Just imagine this woman, only 4 foot 11, having to hit her husband over the head to stop the onslaught. Although my father never beat me, I was the witness to these horrors, and the pain of it all remains seared in my consciousness.

My father died when I was seven. The dire years of dysfunction and that ever-present danger were in the past. My mother, Ruth, who had come from Ukraine as not much more than a child herself, would be figuring out life while raising me—her youngest child—on her own. My brother and sister, 17 and 12 years older than me, respectively, were out of the house. My mom and I had each other, but other than that, we had nothing.

My mother was a seamstress, a seasonal occupation, and jobs were hard to come by in early 1950s Brooklyn. She was always laid off. Every year we were on unemployment insurance. On Wednesdays, we'd go to the unemployment office, and they would give her jobs to go on—sometimes that worked out, many times it did not. Money was always an issue.

If we went out to dinner, it was very special, and we always ordered the least expensive thing on the menu. The only place where we might not order the least expensive entrée was at a Chinese restaurant. My mother liked the shrimp in lobster sauce and spare ribs, and that's what we ate.

As difficult as it seems to imagine such scenes, repainted all these years later, these memories of my mother and shadows of my Brooklyn childhood are always with me. No money, no security, teetering on the economic brink every day. We got through because my mother was strong, she set examples in perseverance, overcoming challenges that seemed insurmountable, giving so that others might have—lifelong lessons that I would embrace.

Yet there was no one to play the role model on other levels, to show me how to find financial success or succeed in business. I was the first member of my family to graduate high school and college. I often wonder why I'm now sitting here in my beautiful apartment, overlooking the East River, and other people are not.

There is no single reason, no one thing. As an investor, however, I believe that success comes down to two things.

One, I understand markets. And two, I took the risk.

Learning to understand markets takes exactly that—learning. You can study and then study some more, explore and test and analyze, and eventually understanding will come. Risk is something else entirely. It speaks more to your personality than to your ability to learn. Yet embracing risk is something you can teach yourself. It starts with looking inside, really examining your feelings and honestly assessing what you're afraid of, recognizing what it is that's preventing you from being a risk taker.

We're all afraid of something. Could be big, could be small, but there's probably something there tugging, gnawing at you. To succeed, you're going to identify it, face it, and come to focus on your strengths. I've seen it time and again, in all walks of life, my own included.

I don't care who you're dealing with—you could be the most confident person in the world, and still, you have to overcome your own fears. Most of us want to be successful, but it's just a question of how to get there. Most people don't know how good they are.

In general, people don't understand their strengths, the expertise they have, the value of the experience they have acquired.

Risk is at the heart of any new venture. Truth be told, it's there in every repeat venture as well. Nothing is guaranteed, no matter how many times you do it. If you want to succeed, you're going to find yourself putting something on the line. You have to be willing to lose something of value. It could be money, it could be your reputation, even your sense of self-worth. Regardless, you must accept the fact that without risk, there's no reward.

Taking risks is not, however, synonymous with being reckless. These are two very different ideas. Smart risk-taking is informed risk-taking. By preparing yourself— whether it's learning a real estate market before buying a house or going over every detail of a case before a trial or training before hiking the slopes of the world's tallest mountain—you'll be successful. Sometimes, the driving force behind your preparation may be fear, or anxiety. And that's okay.

As a lawyer, I over-prepared and I over-prepared. That's why I was considered a good lawyer. But it took its toll on me. I went from one trial to the other, and I was always afraid I was missing something, and I would go to sleep and then wake up and say, Oh, I have to do this memo or I have to do that memo. By the time I hit my 60s, I was physically exhausted.

Yes, even after decades of success in law, real estate investing, launching a landmark TV show and a groundbreaking website, I could be afraid of failure. It may be hard to believe from the outside, looking in. But it's true. It remains a fact today. Every single day, I face a challenge to believe in myself and to push forward.

Deep down inside, I have walls that I have to break. I'm a very conservative person by nature, and I was raised by a very conservative mother, so for me to take these risks, I have to say to myself *I can, I will, I must.*

That's why I've always worked so hard at researching my projects—so I can determine whether I'm looking at a good risk or something I should leave in the rearview mirror. This knowledge helps give me the confidence to take that risk. And there's only one way to get it. *Due Diligence.* By the end of this book, you're going to know those two words intimately.

Due diligence minimizes risk. In business, only take risks after you've done your due diligence. Risk takers with an entrepreneurial spirit are the ones who become financially secure.

Never be scared of failing, never be scared of making mistakes, because it's part of the process of success. Show me a successful person who's willing to fail and I'll show you someone who's on the way to bigger things.

I've never actually endured true failure. That's not because I'm perfect. That's because true failure implies finality, and I believe in the power of never giving up. Failing in one instance only prepares me to succeed the next time around. There have been plenty of mistakes and missteps, but an error at any given moment is the opportunity to apply the learned lesson somewhere else in the future.

Challenges get in the way. They will without a doubt slow you down every now and then. A market will often turn against you before it turns for you. But never let it stop you dead in your tracks. Along Thomas Edison's journey toward changing the world, he told everyone that he didn't fail every time some idea didn't pan out—he merely learned 10,000 ways he could *not* make a light bulb.

So many people are risk averse, afraid of failing, but everybody makes mistakes, everybody fails. It's the successful person who can get off the floor. As Samuel Beckett said, "Ever tried, ever failed. No matter. Try again. Fail again. Fail better." That's how you become successful—you have to persevere.

Look at the great entertainers and performers. How many

auditions did they go to, only to wait around for a call-back that never came? How many songs did they write and rehearse, only to hear people hiss and sneer and tell them they'd never make it? How sick to their stomachs were they the first time they stepped out on stage or in front of a camera, not knowing what would happen? How many people told them they weren't pretty enough, weren't funny enough, weren't young enough, weren't old enough, weren't good enough?

It takes time, it takes commitment, it takes believing in yourself, it takes picking yourself up again and again. You think Jay-Z and Beyoncé didn't face doubts, didn't get rejected plenty of times on their way to fame and becoming my neighbor in the Hamptons? (Yes, it's true.)

It's hard work for a person to realize how good they really are. And who among us appreciates how good we really are? We always feel there's somebody better, somebody who knows more. There's always a better writer, a better lawyer, a better real estate broker. The truth is, people have to embrace how good they really are.

Then the risks won't seem so daunting.

If you're scared of doing the wrong thing, you'll never do anything. So that's why it's important for me to break through my walls with a sledgehammer. I have to play the part of a successful person, even though inside me is this young child who doesn't want to make a mistake, who doesn't want to fail. But if you're scared of failure, you'll never go anywhere.

If you're not willing to fail, stay home with the covers over your head.

CHAPTER 9

IF IT AIN'T BROKER, DON'T FIX IT

When is the last time you made a dinner reservation by speaking directly with a human being? How about when you were planning to book that recent vacation or trying to find the best seats before you got tickets to a play or sporting event—did you seek out a face-to-face interaction then? Was it important to you to speak with another person to research and buy that best-selling book, the new back-to-school clothes, those Egyptian cotton bath towels, that 75-inch TV, those must-have pet de-shedding brush gloves, that package of sour cream and onion flavored crickets…

The answers to the above may fluctuate between "It's been so long I can't remember" to "Just yesterday, but I do it less and less" to "People can help with that kind of stuff?" Automation and the ease of finding information online has moved any number of jobs and tasks to the fringes of interpersonal interaction and, in some cases, out of the realm altogether. Real estate is, as you've read earlier in this book and likely experienced first-hand, one more arena falling into that category. Yet it's without question a business where you're going to put a good deal of effort into creating strong relationships with actual people and working with them, in person, to pursue your goals.

The internet is fabulous for locating and searching out a listing, and it has revolutionized the way real estate is sold. But there's nothing like a real estate broker to augment what you found on the internet and help you in the decision-making process. I'm a broker, and when I go into new areas, I use brokers. Brokers are very important.

The fundamentals of real estate investing were true 200 years ago, are true today and will be true 200 years from today. You can learn from everyone you talk to.

I review up to 15 new projects a day, sometimes as many as 100 a week. That's not an exaggeration for effect or to get you to snap to attention. I make copies of information on the projects for which I'd like to do further due diligence. When I'm really interested, I'll call a broker.

I'll request more information from the broker about a particular project, to get a better grasp on an area. In residential real estate it's the area, the location, it's the school system, the taxes, it's how large a lot you have compared to your neighbor. Then you review what comparable homes have sold for in the area.

Yes, even though I'm a real estate broker myself, I work with brokers local to the market I'm investigating. Brokers are an incredibly valuable resource, and they're there to help you. Go ahead, ring one up. Just because you call a broker and ask him or her to show you a property doesn't mean you have to buy it—not right then and there, and not even in the future. You're simply tapping into their insights and expertise, their knowledge about a particular area and its history, even a specific property, to expand your knowledge base.

Go around with brokers and have them show you all the houses that are available at a particular price point. Ask questions. Get to know the properties so you'll come to understand what type of house is selling in a particular price range.

It's okay to ask at this moment, "Aren't brokers just going to try to sell me a property? Isn't that how they make their money? Can I trust them?"

I am a broker myself, so I can tell you the inside viewpoint. A broker is a salesperson, they make their money selling real estate—99% of brokers are very reputable, honest people who want to improve their client's knowledge and experience. But, always keep in mind: a broker is a salesperson. That's why I like to deal with multiple brokers, never one in particular. That goes against what a lot of people do, but if you deal with three brokers, you get different opinions on everything. You learn from them.

As you're getting to know brokers and learning from them, they're getting to know you as well. This is a relationship, after all, a two-way street. Each time you go see a property with them, every time you ask a question or express a concern, they're gleaning knowledge about you and your real estate interests. Over time, they should be able to not only provide you access to the properties you've discovered on your own, but also to those that may be off your radar.

Usually you'll see a property you like in a certain area and you'll call the broker, and that's how the process starts. As you work with that broker, he or she will learn the type of project you like. Maybe they'll know of a property that isn't formally listed, but the owner might be amenable to selling. It's "off market," which means it isn't listed but the seller will sell at the right price.

If you didn't know that brokers can do this type of thing, you're not alone. But now you know. You've acquired knowledge. Everything in the real estate investing world is a learning experience. There's so much to learn. And you never stop learning.

Right now, you're going to learn some lingo.

What is a real estate agent?

An agent is an individual who has taken the minimum number of classes and passed the requisite exams in his or her state. This is an all-encompassing title, under which you'll find brokers, associate brokers, salespeople, etc.

What's the difference between an agent and a broker?

A broker has taken additional classes and has passed a broker's license exam, and has completed a state-mandated amount of time working in the field. Brokers are legally allowed to work on their own, or they may hire agents to work with them. An agent who hasn't passed the broker's exam *must* work with a licensed broker.

What is a REALTOR®?

REALTOR® is actually a registered trademark. It encompasses those individuals who have become members of the National Association of REALTORS® and have agreed to uphold the standards of that organization and its code of ethics. You don't have to join this organization to operate as an agent or broker.

What is a listing broker? And why do you want one?

A listing broker is hired by the seller to do the obvious: sell their property. They create marketing and advertising plans, and they know everything there is to know about a property—including how to help the seller connect with the right buyer.

I have one steadfast rule when it comes to working with agents and brokers:

You always want to deal with the listing broker.

Why?

First of all, the listing broker has the most information about their particular listing. Second, if you go to another broker, the listing broker has to share his or her commission with the other broker. You want to go right to the listing broker because there's more of an incentive to sell you the house—because they get not just 50% of the fee if they work directly with you and no other broker, they get 100%. And they know the product. Always try to deal only with the listing broker, when you can.

When you go on a site like Zillow, you're going to see a sea of names and faces all seemingly associated with every listing. Instinct might tell you to go with the one on the very top. With brokers, sometimes it pays to start at the bottom.

When I look on Zillow, since I only want to deal with the listing broker, I go to bottom of the page. On the top of the page on the right-hand side are brokers who are sponsored advertisers—some people think they're the listing brokers, but they're not. On Zillow, at the bottom of the page it will say "Listed by x, y, z broker or brokerage." That's the one you want to deal with.

Your Broker and You

When you're choosing a professional to work with,

whether it's a doctor, a lawyer, an accountant or a real estate broker, you have to be proactive. When you go to a doctor and they give you a diagnosis of, say, surgery or another serious course of treatment, usually you'll want to get another opinion. Or maybe you'll go to the internet and research the topic and then go ask both the original doctor and another physician follow-up questions. You want to get to the heart of the decision-making process.

So when a broker tells you something, go to the internet and research the topic. One, the research may tell you that you're asking the wrong questions. Two, it may help you realize that the broker you're asking may not be the broker for you to buy with on this particular project.

You always want to go to a broker who you think is knowledgeable and experienced in that specific area, and the particular segment of real estate you're interested in.

What do we mean by segment? Is it residential or commercial? Are you looking to buy a building with existing businesses or to start something new in an empty space? Let's say you're looking to buy land and build a house—that's a different project than just buying a property with a house already on it. So in that case, you'll want to go to a broker who has a deep knowledge of land.

Along with that, they have to know zoning. Why? To help you understand what you can and can't do as a developer, to aid in discovering challenges earlier in your search rather than later. Take an area like the Hamptons, where there are bays and ponds and rivers and the ocean to contend with. Somebody who has worked in the area for years—brokering lots on which all levels of homes have been constructed—will know things about the property that might otherwise take you a long time to discover. Sometimes, buyers learn things too late, things that can take a plan south before you even get started. You want a broker who won't let that happen.

In the Hamptons, for example, a broker would need to know if there are wetlands on a property. In many jurisdictions, you have to go through a wetlands commission to determine what the requirements are to build on a lot. In fact, the lot may not be buildable at all, because it's so close to, or actually within, an area designated as wetlands.

Wetlands are just one of the potential roadblocks you may face in rural and suburban areas. In cities, there are urban planning rules and other factors you'll uncover if that becomes your area of interest. Your internet research and your interactions with numerous expert brokers will fuel your knowledge and understanding. Remember, it will take time, effort and analysis.

Do this, and within three to four months you'll be amazed at how much information you've gained by going to open houses, by seeing listings, even by making low offers.

Making offers, Alan? Are you sure about that?

Yes, I am sure. And I say "making low offers" intentionally. After all, how will you know how much a seller will really take until you make an offer? This is part of the information-gathering process. As many times as you'll make an offer, they'll come back to what they'll really take—and it may be 5%, 7% or even 8 % less than what they're asking.

Now you're learning a market. And once you learn the market, then you're getting a feel. *I'm not necessarily in the market, but I'm learning the market* you'll say to yourself. You're not necessarily saying you're financially able to buy it, but remember, that's the last thing. Money is the last thing. You're gaining something much more valuable at this stage: knowledge and confidence in your ability to learn a market.

You have to go see it, feel it, touch it. And once you do that, then all of a sudden you're learning. And then one day a broker calls you or you see *IT* on the internet—a house that you believe is selling for less than market value—and there's a buying opportunity!

CHAPTER 10

NOBODY PUTS ALAN IN A CORNER

Investing in real estate is not a hobby. This is a business you're preparing to enter. It may not be your only business, but make no mistake, it will be *yours*. You will own it, define it, expand it and thrive in it. And that will take an entrepreneurial spirit.

Whether you know it or not, you probably already have that spirit—it may flow freely out of you or you might need a little help coaxing it into the open. If you know it's there, and how to tap into it, good for you. That's a plus. If you're not so sure, well, chances are you've let it loose at least once or twice. Could have been last week, could have been years ago. But there was probably a sign.

You've come this far, so it's there somewhere. Take a look.

Understand that it doesn't necessarily have to have anything to do with real estate, or whatever profession in which you may currently find yourself engaged. It isn't tied to any specific product or field or business. Rather, it's a state of mind. It's an approach that encompasses educating yourself and facing challenges, building skills and applying your strengths into a whole new aspect of life at some point.

My entrepreneurship started when I was 16 years old. I got a job as a busboy in Atlantic City, New Jersey with two of my closest friends during the Passover-Easter break. Malcolm and Marty were the waiters, because they were taller, and I was the busboy. Then that summer, the three of us—Malcolm, Marty and I—got jobs waiting tables in the Catskills.

The Catskill Mountains, home to Kutscher's and the Nevele, Grossinger's and the Concord. These were household names to New Yorkers from the 1920s through the 1980s, famous resorts that offered family vacations a few hours north of Manhattan and, in a film that captured the glory days of this unforgettable summertime getaway culture, made *Dirty Dancing* a phenomenon. There were people to meet, money to be made and opportunities to grab hold of for a bold and hardworking young man willing to put himself out there. And nobody puts Alan in a corner.

I worked 16 hours a day at Charlow's Irvington Hotel, serving meals during the children's shift, then did double shifts as the staff waiter for the adults. That's six meals a day, six days a week. In the afternoon I sold soda at the pool. And then about three times a week, I ran the bingo games. And I did some work in the nightclub—it was actually more like a casino with a comedian—in the evening, bussing tables. There were six of us sharing a room the size of a closet, and we had bunk beds. I was on the bottom, and the guy above me had to weigh 350 pounds. When he would get in, the mattress would sink right to my nose. If I got up to go to the bathroom, when I got back I had to go in sideways. That was the hardest I ever worked in my life.

I was also a talker, a "people person" before the term even existed, and the job helped me hone a love of simply engaging with people, a skill that has buoyed me in every business venture. Listening to others, helping them get what they need—that will take you places, and it makes whatever journey you're on all the more rewarding. That is part of the spirit we were talking about a few paragraphs ago.

Many of these personality traits were honed from a young age, and it was anything but accidental. Early on in life, emotional pain was my catalyst for change. One particular childhood memory has the caustic bite of a fresh wound, still a bit raw.

I was in eighth grade. I was outside my friend's house, and there was a porch, and I heard my friends talking about me. They were talking about forming a club, and I would be excluded from the club. I stood there listening to the conversation, I stood there for a long time, absolutely devastated. Rejected by my friends.

I remember, the next day was the Ohio Exams, and I'd always been in the top percentages on these kinds of tests, but on this occasion I did very far from my best. To be rejected by my friends, and to be listening to their conversation as they were rejecting me in secret, to me, was the end of the world.

There must have been a group of four or five boys, and I went around to each and every one of them individually. I went to their houses, and I wanted to know what it was about me that they didn't like. Each one told me why they voted me out of the club. One person told me that whenever I talked, I actually touched him—like when some people talk, they'll hold your arm or your shoulder. So I stopped touching people entirely. To this day, frankly, I don't like people touching me, either. It was very interesting, looking back. I made a complete personality change at that young age, because it was so devastating.

A few years later, I graduated Tilden High School and was off to college. We had no money whatsoever, so I went to a tuition-free school, Brooklyn College. And I started a business selling sweatshirts and T-shirts to the fraternities and sororities. No matter where you go to school, not all learning happens in the classroom.

Everything they wore had to have their name on it, whether it was Phi Sigma or Delta house. I contracted with a firm in Manhattan that did silk screening. I'd get an order and then

I would silk screen it with the name of the fraternity or the sorority, and I did that throughout my college years.

Eventually I enlisted sales people at the other colleges all through New York. But it's a big country, and those Greek letters weren't going to get on all those sweatshirts by themselves. There was no Amazon, so I went mail order.

I made up a brochure, put Campus Apparel Incorporated right there on the front, and sent out 1,000 of them.

Nothing.

Not five, not two, not one. Zero response. And then I sent out another one, and I got maybe five, and another one, and I got maybe 10, and then I kept sending them out, and little by little it became a good business. I was selling all over the country by mail order.

All the orders earned me the spending money to get through four undergraduate years. It taught me how to create and manage a business, how to get and then hold onto clients, the art of sales and customer service, the power of marketing one's product and oneself. And, as with all experiences, it proffered a bit of wisdom I would carry forward.

My brother-in-law worked for Kayser-Roth, a sock and hosiery company. They were very large, a New York Stock Exchange company. I bought a gross of stockings—144 pairs of stockings—and I figured I could sell them because I worked with all these women's groups. Unfortunately, at the same time that I did this, pantyhose came out.

So let it be said that the women in my family were wearing these stockings for years. That taught me a lesson—do your due diligence and know your market.

CHAPTER 11

ROCKY MOUNTAIN HIGH

The last remnants of summer are blowing off Main Street in Southampton as small crowds bustle on the sidewalk. It's not uncommon on these bricks to see flashbulbs popping around the likes of Sofia Vergara or Leonardo DiCaprio, but now the glitterati glow of Hamptons high season has given way to a certain vibe of languorous calm.

Still, as I sit in this restaurant and dine with a friend, some of the most desired real estate in the world—oceanfront homes on endless strands of white, mansions hiding behind hedges—is within walking distance from where we're eating. And that, to me, is an energizing force.

We're chatting about my favorite maxim of investing: If a market goes up 8% a year, over a 20-year period or more, you know that's a good project. Good areas only get better.

A few heads at nearby tables turn slightly, seeming to listen in, perhaps looking for some free investing advice. (If you're reading this and remember being there, congratulations on making it into the book!) In any case, eavesdroppers and everyone else should know, I practice what I preach.

When I bought in Aspen, Colorado, for instance, I did my

study, and saw over the long term that the market went up double digits a year. How could I go wrong? I didn't. And it turned out that was a wonderful real estate area.

Aspen. Home to the most expensive real estate in the country. Looking at it, even the Hamptons might have to attribute some of that green hue coloring the hedgerows and rolling lawns to envy.

I always wanted to have a getaway in the mountains. We had something by the seashore, we lived in town, but I always wanted something in the mountains. So, with both business and pleasure in mind, I went with my family for a week's vacation to ski in Aspen.

Before that I'd been looking in other ski areas out west, like Park City, Utah. Aspen was not an artificial ski town, like Vail (where I looked also), which was made to ski. Aspen was a real town, and a beautiful town, with its own history.

On my second or third day there, I was running around and I saw they were building a project right in the core, right downtown, one block from the gondola, which takes you to the top of the mountain. It was 10 townhomes. I asked one of the workmen if I could take a look. "Knock yourself out," he said.

It was the model, and I really liked it, so I went across the street to the nearest brokerage, I went to the reception desk, and I said I'd like to see a broker. A woman came out and I asked, "Do you have the listing of the townhouse across the street?"

"I do," she said.

"I'd like to buy one," I said.

"Fine," she said. And eventually it ended up in a sale, and she was very happy.

Well, as any good story goes, maybe it was a little more complicated than that.

So, the next day I came back with my wife and the broker to the model house, because I wanted to meet the builder. The builder already knew I was very interested and I was coming back for a second visit.

I was talking with the builder, trying to negotiate—I like to do my negotiating myself, I don't have to negotiate through a broker—and he says, "Alan, do you see that man over there? Well, that man just gave me a check on this unit."

I said, "Boy, what a coincidence."

He said, "No, it's not a coincidence, he's been looking at this unit and negotiating with me for six months, and when I told him that you were coming back, and that you had been here twice before, once with a broker and once on your own, and you were a serious buyer, it put a fire under him. And he gave me a check. So this unit is no longer available."

I said, "No problem, you have other units, right?" And he said yes.

"I see your other units haven't been built yet," I said.

"That's correct," he said.

I said, "No problem, I'll buy one that's not built." And he said, that's no problem, Alan, but it's going to be $100,000 more.

"Well, is it larger?" I asked.

No.

"Does it have other amenities?"

Again, no.

"Let me see if I understand this," I said. "If I had come here two hours earlier, before this gentleman was here, and had given you my check at that time—it was one o'clock, so if I came here at 10:30, you'd have taken my check and I would have gotten the unit. Is that correct?"

"Absolutely," he said.

"It's now one o'clock, and you're telling me the next unit— which is identical to this unit—is $100,000 more?"

"Correct," he said.

I told him I needed to think about it. I felt like I'd just lost $100,000. I did it again—I waited too long. Had I given him a check the day before or earlier...

That night, I had a conversation with myself. Did I really want to pay $100,000 more for this unit? First, I had to go through a process: Was it worth it? The location couldn't be better, the units are beautiful, 4,000 square feet, double garage, great location, all brick—yeah, it's worth it.

And then I wondered, "Can you swallow your pride and pay this man an extra $100,000?" I thought, "It's going to be very hard."

"But can you do it?"

"Reluctantly," I thought.

"Alright, so do it," I said.

But due diligence had to be done first. I spent the next few days seeing every Aspen property in that suddenly elevated price range. Then I went back to New York and analyzed the situation. In Colorado, you have 20 days to back out of a contract, and on day 19 I awoke, told my wife I was going to Aspen to view the house and location again, and got on a plane.

That afternoon, after seeing the location and the model house, I was confident it was a valid deal. I called Judy and said, "I am coming back home. I like the deal." I came home the next day. The rest is history.

Aspen remains the farthest distance that any investment lies from my Manhattan home base. I remember distinctly how brokers told me "the waters were very, very cold in Aspen, and you don't want to jump into the water"—comparing it to real estate, because it's so pricey. But you know what? Once you jump in, you get used to the water, you get used to the cold, and it's just fine.

So fine that I still own that same unit, and it's worth at least five times what I paid for it. What fascinates me is how the demographics have changed over the quarter-century since I took the plunge. The people who bought there before were professionals, people like myself. And now in my development, because it's so well located, right by the gondola, there are Fortune 500 CEOs and hedge fund magnates, some of the richest people in the world, who are my neighbors.

So if you're thinking to yourself that it's too late to buy in Aspen, that you've missed the boat on that kind of appreciation, read on...

CHAPTER 12

THE BEST TIME TO BUY
REAL ESTATE IS...

Timing, they say, is everything.

One of the questions people always seem to ask, no matter the time of year or time of day, the state of the weather or the height or depth of the stock market, is...

When is the best time to buy real estate?

I will tell you.

Now.

The answer is now.

NOW IS A GOOD TIME TO BUY REAL ESTATE. It's as loud and clear and simple as that.

You haven't really heard the answer and you're probably already following up with another question: How can you give an unequivocal *Now*, followed by a no-ifs-ands-or-buts *It's a good time to buy real estate*, if that question can be asked any place, at any time?

It's simple. It's always a good time to buy real estate...if you have the right location. And the right attitude.

That's all you need. But it's *exactly* what you need. Nothing less is going to work.

You can time certain things in life. When to get out of bed in the morning so you can get to work on time. When to fly to Hawaii. When to take the chicken out of the oven. You time those things. But you do not time real estate investing—at least not if you want to maximize your chances at being successful. Sure, there are countless websites, online courses and books offering to teach you precisely that, how to intuit the perfect time to enter the market and the exact moment to get out. I don't subscribe to those theories. Never have. Consider this your fair warning.

Simply put, there's nobody out there smart enough to accurately time something as complex as the housing market. If I knew the right time to buy real estate, we wouldn't be living in New York City right now, we'd be living in Schnurmanville. More to the point, having a "right time" to buy real estate is an irrelevant concept, because you're in it for the long term.

Take in those two words for just a moment. *Long term.*

You're not going to buy a property today and sell it tomorrow. You're looking to get into a good market and stay there. That's how you're going to make money.

In a good market, prices go up and up. A fallacy I always hear is, *Oh my god, prices are so high, they can't go higher. It's just ridiculous.* Wrong.

I've made two types of mistakes as a real estate investor. I never made a mistake in buying anything. I've only made mistakes in selling too soon and not holding on to a property. Or I had a contract, I was considering buying something, and I should have bought it but I didn't go through with it.

I have drawers full of two things: properties that I didn't buy and they've tripled in value, and properties I've sold and they've subsequently gone up 10 times. But in real estate, true professionals never look back.

Well, that's only partially true. I never look back with a sense of regret, but I'll take a glance into the rearview mirror when it provides a learning moment.

One night many years ago, I went to a restaurant called Bubby's in Tribeca. On my walk there, I saw a little sign on a building that said it was for sale. It looked intriguing, so I called the number and left a message, but never heard anything. Then, two weeks later, the broker called back. He said he'd gotten so many calls that he was returning each one in order, and he'd finally gotten to me.

The building was in terrible condition both inside and out,

and it came with a $6.8 million price tag. But it was a great location, right off Hudson Street, and it oozed potential. So I called up my partners, they agreed to go for it, and after a bidding war we paid $7.2 million.

We sold it nine months later for $9 million, that guy sold it for $12 million, then the next guy sold it for $16 million. So what do I know?

In another deal not long after, my partners and I acquired another Manhattan building—this one had 32 apartments and 5 stores—for $19 million, then sold it for $31 million after owning it for six or seven years, drawing income the whole time. Not a bad return on investment, right? Well, guess what the new owner did with the property? He sold the stores for $19 million—just the five stores alone—and then he sold the apartments above for something in the ballpark of $28 million.

So he got $47 million, he gave us $31 million. I wish I was as smart as that guy!

Still, I never say, "I should have done this, I should have done that." I learn from the experience and move along. When I sell a project that the other person makes a lot of money on, the first thing I say is, Good for them!

The point is, when it comes to well-located real estate, if you liked the price when you bought it, that's all there is to it. You probably didn't buy at the bottom. That's okay. It would be foolish to think you could plan such an event. And if you're patient, chances are you'll be pleased with the price if and when you eventually sell it.

It may sound like hyperbole, but in real estate, the sky *is* the limit—particularly in places like New York City, Aspen and the Hamptons. Prices will always rise, because there's always people being born, there's people always moving into these sought-after zip codes—there's always demand. And real estate is just like high school economics. It's all about supply and demand. When there's more supply than demand, the market gets soft. When there's more demand than supply, the market gets more robust and goes up.

For example, in the past we've seen a flattening of the market in an area like the Hamptons, because at one point there were hundreds of homes built on spec, more than the market could absorb in a short time period. So the market gets quiet. Buyers have so many choices, they're suddenly in no rush to buy. The ones who are buying are getting what they consider a value buy—some builders will have challenges in making their payments, investors will want to get out of the deal, the builder doesn't want to lose his home to the bank.

Naturally, prices may even continue to fall after you buy. They may be rising right this very second and you'll pay more tomorrow than you would right this second. Who knows what will happen tomorrow? So there are no demerits at this moment if you're thinking to yourself, *But don't I want to wait to buy at the moment things are softest, so they can go up? Isn't that the time to buy? And what if that time isn't right now?*

Remember, nobody can tell you the future, so you'll never know if you're at the absolute top or bottom. And you shouldn't try to find, or to become, a soothsayer. When we bought our Manhattan apartment in the early 1990s, we sold our Park Slope home for $805,000, without a broker. If you recall, I bought it for $120,000. A nice profit, indeed, so it must have been a smart move, right?

Of course, we should have kept it—today it's worth $4.5 million.

Before I lived in Manhattan, I invested there. I started with a condominium in a brand new building at 630 First Avenue, a complex called Manhattan Place. It was a one-bedroom condo but could have been a two bedroom in a pinch, 1,000 square feet with a beautiful view of the river. I paid $330,000 and immediately rented it out for $2,400 a month, covering all my expenses. Years later, I sold it for $825,000 to one of my tenants.

Two more condominiums followed. The second one was called the Promenade at 76th Street and the East River, a one-bedroom with a river view. The third, another one-bedroom at 79th Street and First Avenue, was, perhaps prophetically, in a building called Hampton House. Both were in the $300,000 range, a price I paid because of their location and what I believed it meant for their potential value. Should I have bought earlier? Later? Irrelevant.

Well, not entirely. One caveat. When evaluating an investment, you must consider not if it's a *good time* to enter the real estate market, but rather if it's *a good time for you* to enter the real estate market. That's a question only you can answer.

You may be shocked by this, but you're not going to start that self-analysis with money. Evaluating the finances is the last thing you should consider. Not the first, the last.

CHAPTER 13

WHEN I'M CRYIN' I SHOULD BE BUYIN'

The stock market isn't my world of choice, as by now you know. But that doesn't mean there aren't lessons to be learned in the land of bears and bulls that can be applied to real estate investing. Quite the contrary. In fact, one of my favorite aphorisms was born out of watching how Wall Street's best behave during its bleakest hours.

In the stock market, they say you should buy when there's blood in the street. Well, the same holds true for any market, real estate included. When you feel things are only going to get worse, and you read articles saying things like "Single Family Home Ownership Is Dead in the United States Forever," ask yourself, What do they know?

The answer? They know nothing. There are always people being born, populations are always rising, and if you have a good location, it's usually going to be getting better, not worse. So I use the expression, "When I'm cryin', I should be buyin'."

Put it on your coffee mug. When I'm Cryin', I Should Be Buyin'.

I don't know exactly when I came up with it, but it had to be around the time I fully realized that real estate was cyclical. Every market in the world is cyclical. You show me one market that goes straight up—it just doesn't work that way.

Over time, I truly realized how real estate works: The market keeps going up, and builders and entrepreneurs are buying real estate, and contractors and builders are building new real estate—they're building new apartments, new homes, because the market keeps going up and they want to take advantage.

But what happens is they build *so* much, they buy *so* much, they raise prices *so* much during the buying and building frenzy that something happens. They price themselves above what a particular area, the people in that area, the economics in that area, can sustain.

Real estate markets are extremely efficient. When too many houses are being built—because there's a finite number of people who can buy a particular house in a particular location at a particular price—it's a supply situation. So when there's more supply than demand, when a market gets so frothy that the price of a particular house, apartment or commercial property exceeds the economics of the area—because all real estate is local—then you have a whipsaw reaction.

And what is that reaction? People stop renting, people stop buying, and that new house or apartment just sits vacant.

Meanwhile, the entrepreneur or the landlord is incurring expenses—interest expenses on the new construction, real estate taxes on that new construction, real estate taxes on the building where he's trying to rent an apartment.

The property sits there, and after four, five, six months, that entrepreneur realizes he must offer some type of incentive to a potential buyer. And what greater incentive than a price reduction? In an apartment, if the owner wants to maintain the rental price, he might offer two months free rent. If it's a condominium, a buyer might get condo dues paid for a year. If it's a house, the seller might provide upgrades—because the goal is to maintain a particular price point on the house. That way, when it comes time to sell the next one, he can say, "I sold house x for this much, and this house is a carbon copy."

Yes, eventually something will sell. Because it must. Few people can simply wait out the storm. In a down market, when the economy cannot sustain the pricing seen during the up market, there are people who still have to sell. I call this group the DDB.

Death. Divorce. Bankruptcy.

Remember, when the volume of transfers in an area goes way down, that becomes the market. And there is this group of people, the DDB, who are willing to take less, because their circumstances have forced the issue. They have to sell, and they can't wait for things to improve. Since real estate pricing is based on comps—what did a similar house sell for in a similar area at a particular price point (as you learned in "How to Find Your Market")—these lower prices being accepted by the DDB crowd bring down the comps in that area, and thus the local real estate market goes down.

So what happens now? What should you, the savvy investor, do? Recognize the opportunity—that's what! In down real estate markets, in a place like the Hamptons, Aspen or Palm Beach, most of the people who own real estate are substantial people and it's a boutique society, so when the market softens, they generally don't sell. They hold, because most sophisticated investors know it's not a selling opportunity, it's a buying opportunity.

And the up-down-up-down cycle will go just that way again and again over time.

Two years have gone by, three years have gone by, there's very little volume, builders are not building, speculators are not building rental apartments, people are not building commercial buildings, but there's always some demand. The economy picks up, prices have fallen, the stock market has leveled off, and now all of a sudden you find there's *more demand* three years down the pike than supply. What happens where there's more demand than supply? The existing inventory gets absorbed, then there isn't enough inventory to meet the demand, and prices start rising.

Good thing you were paying attention in high school economics. That supply-and-demand thing is going to come in very handy in your real estate journey, especially when you find yourself in a market where teardrops, along with prices, are falling around you.

When the market goes down it's usually a buying opportunity, if there's nothing else truly going on in the economy other than the normal up-and-down cycle of any commodity. And real estate is a commodity. So when I came up with the expression "When I'm Cryin', I Should Be Buyin'," what that really means is that in a market that's going through a contraction or a consolidation, there's opportunity—and it's the professionals who take advantage of the opportunity.

Pros always keep substantial cash reserves in order to get through down markets, to be able to feed a project that might need time to evolve, but they also use those reserves to take advantage of opportunities that present themselves. Again, this applies whether you're investing on Main Street or Wall Street.

When there's a consolidation phase in the stock market— which is very healthy—and it goes down 460 points in one morning, pros smell blood in the water. They know the market is flushing itself. The weak money is out there selling to the strong money.

If you're a seller, you want to be selling when the market is hitting new highs every day, when people are lining up to buy your property, when nothing can go wrong. A lot of people will go, "No, it's going up, it will go up higher!" That's the time to sell.

You sell in good times, you buy in bad times. There's no secret to that. It's always better to buy when things are going down. But nobody wants to catch that falling knife. Everybody wants to buy when things are going up. But professionals know that everything is a market, and you buy low and sell high. People will be saying, *Oh my god, the market is going lower, the market is going lower.* And that may well be true.

I received a call one day from one of my best friends, who was looking to purchase an apartment in Manhattan. He told me he had just read an article in *The Wall Street Journal* saying that prices were going down and that some sellers were accepting offers below their purchase price. He asked me what to do. I told him, "I am not at all interested in today's newspaper article on market conditions. I want to read tomorrow's paper."

You're never going to reach the top and never hit the bottom, but it's that middle section that's going to send your kids to college, that middle section where you can buy your retirement home, that middle section that will lead you to a feeling of financial security.

CHAPTER 14

OPTIMISM IS THE FAITH
THAT LEADS TO ACHIEVEMENT

I always order tea. Regardless of the season, a pot of water and a sachet of tea leaves are coming to the table. The process of steeping, slow and organic and reliable, the patience required in its making, suits me. There's something steadier about tea, something more in balance with the ebb and flow of time, than almost any other beverage.

You may also catch me drinking a glass of water on occasion. Not that the beverage itself really matters. I've never been served a glass that's half empty at any restaurant in the world. I learned long ago that in order to be able to accomplish anything in this life, you must have a positive outlook.

In the mid 1990s, a friend of mine who I'd known since sophomore year in high school sent me a note. He put a number of quotes on it, knowing that I was always interested in such things. I read through them, then stopped cold at the last one on the page.

"Optimism is the faith that leads to achievement. Nothing can be done without hope and confidence." —Helen Keller

When I read it, I said *Oh my god.* Nobody has had challenges like Helen Keller, and I immediately wrote those words down.

Write them down yourself. Underline or highlight them right now, right here on this page. Say them out loud. Listen to them.

Optimism is the faith that leads to achievement. Nothing can be done without hope and confidence.

Optimism and confidence. That's how you become successful, that's how you achieve. You have to have confidence in yourself—where are you going without that? And you have to be optimistic. So I took that quote and I embraced it.

Many years before I read those wise words, I did my best to live them, deliberately. Think positively and act upon it. That's not necessarily an innate behavior, and there will likely be forces in your life pushing in the opposite direction. In my childhood, these destructive forces were all around me, and I was determined not to allow them to undermine my dreams.

My family was so dysfunctional. My brother and sister and I had challenges, coming from such a violent environment. My family was always used to failure. They were not used to success. They didn't know how to deal with success.

I was always determined to take another path. And yet

when I had success, I felt neither the need nor desire to tell others what I was doing. I kept my own confidence. Some people feel the need to talk about all their victories to anyone who will listen. I simply did it, told myself I could keep doing it, and moved forward with a faith that I never could have mustered back in that Brooklyn apartment of my youth.

Coming out of that type of home, I don't know what made me different. I think it was because after my father died, it was just my mother and me. She used to call me "My Alan." Everything was, "My Alan this" and "My Alan that." Here's a woman who stood up to a man who was physically abusive to her—to this day, I could never ever lift my hand to anyone—and it was so traumatic, seeing such abuse as a child. She gave me the confidence that I could do anything.

Optimism is the faith that leads to achievement. Nothing can be done without hope and confidence.

Not every deal is going to work out. Not every dream becomes a reality. Not every plan comes to fruition. But you have to have confidence to strive.

A positive approach is exactly that—an *approach*. To strive, in and of itself, does not mean to achieve. It simply means you're moving in your desired direction. When you're searching the internet day after day for properties and nothing comes up, when you're looking through house after house and not finding one that makes sense for you, you have to maintain hope that you'll find what you're searching for—or that you'll find something you didn't know you were looking for, but that sparks your interest and eventually turns out to be a great deal. If you believe in your vision, if you find an area that—after you've done your due diligence—you believe is a good investment, then you'll have courage in your convictions.

You can't be in real estate and not be optimistic. If you're not optimistic, this isn't for you. So when I say that Helen Keller phrase, I say it and I believe it. I have to believe that if I buy a property, good things will happen. And I prove it. And I prove it and I prove it and I prove it.

This approach has worked for me in real estate for decades. But the same philosophy holds true no matter what you want to do. Want to launch a clothing line or a restaurant? Want to write a book or make a movie? Want to open a shop that sells plastic pink flamingos and chocolate croissants? Have hope. Believe you can do it. Jeff Bezos, Steve Jobs, Steven Spielberg and Warren Buffett didn't bring their visions to reality by doubting themselves.

That family who's owned the bakery on the corner for the past four generations, that columnist you read every day, that actor you see in every one of his movies because he makes you laugh? They didn't do it overnight. They didn't succeed on their very first day. Or their second. Their paths were doubtless paved by setbacks, challenges, hurdles and dark moments of doubt. Yet they kept telling themselves they would make it, they could do it, they *would* do it.

I've never met an entrepreneur who isn't optimistic. How can you start a factory, a new job, how can you start any new endeavor? How can you push boundaries, how can you develop land that you've never developed before, how can you buy a hotel, which you've never done before, if you're not optimistic?

The answer is, you can't.

That's why I have "I can, I will, I must. I can, I will, I must." Inside me, there are many insecurities—just like there are in every single person in the world—but if you think *I can, I will, I must, I can, I will, I must,* then you can overcome that self-doubt. Combine that with optimism, with a good attitude, and you're a long way toward having a successful life. You could do a lot worse than to follow those tenets.

CHAPTER 15

ALL HAIL THE TAXI

This is the way summer days were meant to be spent: top down in my car, sun shining, cruising through Sagaponack and Bridgehampton, gazing at the architectural and natural wonders that are Hamptons real estate. There's both a tangible, unhurried air and a nod to social and historical context as you drive past—slowing ever-so-slightly—the homes of, say, a major book company CEO, a former star NFL quarterback and a host of others.

I've driven friends and clients on these roads, pointing out landmarks and highlights in the surroundings, and have been told more than once, "You'd be a great cab driver." Usually, I laugh, and days gone by are suddenly not as far in the rearview mirror as they might appear.

As popular as my T-shirts and sweatshirts may have been in the fraternities and sororities, casual collegiate clothing and the promise of keeping the Greek system swathed in something other than togas were not going to be my alpha and omega. Running Campus Apparel had taught me how to create and manage a business, how to get and then hold onto clients, the art of sales and customer service, the power of marketing one's product and oneself. And of course it had provided something of a financial flotilla during those undergraduate years.

But morning glances in the mirror each day did not return the reflections that, say, a Ralph Lauren or a Donna Karan or a Tommy Hilfiger might have seen. When I entered law school, nearly two decades before Champion elevated the collegiate sweatshirt to the stuff of high, or at least highly lucrative and oversized, fashion, I left my clothing business behind.

I could not do the same with my financial needs. I had a studio apartment for $106 a month in Manhattan, on 75th Street, right off Central Park West—I wish I still had that rent-controlled apartment—and I needed money to live. In those days, the Help Wanted sections were filled with possibilities for somebody unafraid of hard work. I could have waited tables, or been a delivery guy. Sometimes, though, the simplest choice is the right one. The easiest was to drive a cab.

Nearly every weeknight, I'd put 8 to 10 hours on the meter. I would sleep for four or five hours, then I'd go to class. And I did that for three years. During the week I worked Times Square, and that was so exciting. Here I am, this young kid going to Times Square—you get a fare in Times Square, you'd take them somewhere else and then go back to Times Square, because that's where you could always get a fare. You'd get the theater crowd, and after that the nightclub crowd.

Remember, this was 1968. *Taxi Driver* was still eight years from searing Martin Scorsese's vision and Robert De Niro's "Are You Talkin' to Me?" mantra onto the public consciousness. Today, in the comparatively sanitized world of Uber and Lyft, some of the shine that once danced off the chrome of New York City taxis has dulled. Back then, to be at the helm of a cab had a tinge of romance.

There was something about being behind the wheel of that yellow car, the skyscrapers and city lights of the Big Apple rising up as you'd wend your way through the streets of Manhattan. During the week I'd take the night shift, starting at four o'clock. On weekends I worked the daytime. The 30 or so fares I'd get on a typical shift would net me about $3 an hour.

It wasn't just about the money, though. There were other benefits to be had, other skills to be honed and experiences to savor.

I enjoy being around people, I enjoy conversations, I enjoy learning from people. Sometimes you meet someone who's somewhat dysfunctional, and you try to avoid them, but for the most part people are very friendly.

Today, you get in a cab and nobody says anything. But this was the '60s, and people spoke to one another in those days. Cab drivers spoke to you. You'd learn all about them and their countries, and you could show them things that you knew.

One night I even picked up Walter Cronkite.

Now, let's pause a quick moment here. If you're a reader of a certain age, the notion of picking up Mr. Cronkite has most likely already inspired raised highbrows and widened eyes. If you were born after, say, Ronald Reagan left office, you're forgiven it you don't immediately understand that having Walter Cronkite in your cab would be the equivalent of…well, there might actually not be an equivalent in this day and age.

Cronkite was bigger than life. A broadcast journalist when the term wasn't a punch line or contradiction in terms but rather an honored and respected position. He was a source of news, comfort, authority and perspective during some of the most tumultuous years and events on American history. As a reporter in print, radio and TV, he covered every major event from World War II and the Nuremberg Trials to the Vietnam War to Watergate to the Iran Hostage Crisis. As the anchor of the *CBS Evening News* for 20 years, he became as much a part of America's cultural fabric as any other individual. His was the voice and presence that carried a nation through the unfolding horrors of the JFK assassination and the triumphs of the space program as Neil Armstrong walked on the moon.

I knew it was him immediately. Of course, I said, "Hello, Mr. Cronkite, I'm honored to have you in my cab," and I drove him home. I think he lived on 84th or 85th street and

East End Avenue in Manhattan. And I asked him what it was like to be one of the most respected people in the United States, which he was at that time.

Cronkite enjoyed fame and fortune, influence and respect, the admiration of an entire nation regardless of political persuasion. He was named the most trusted man in America in a 1972 poll, an honor that remains associated with his name to this day. That's some kind of legacy to rub shoulders with.

Years later, we wound up living in the same building, and I used to see him in the elevator. Of course, the first time I saw him, I reminded him that he was in my cab when I was a student in law school.

Perhaps more than anything, the cab became a classroom on wheels. I learned the entire city—Bronx, Brooklyn, Queens—from inside that car, building a familiarity with neighborhoods and the flow of the boroughs that would one day inform my forays into New York City real estate.

I also learned patience, which was a very valuable commodity. Because if you don't have patience driving a taxi in heavy traffic, you simply can't do it. It'll drive you crazy. So, to sit in that cab, relax and practice the art of patience—that has served me very, very well. Not only as a lawyer, because sometimes you go to court and have to wait hours to be called in for a conference, but it taught me patience in investing, to always invest for the long term.

On the day I graduated from law school, I went out to a family dinner in downtown New York City to celebrate. My brother-in-law had driven to the restaurant, but for whatever reason he couldn't take me back to my apartment on the Upper West Side. I stood there alone on the city street as he pulled away, arms laden with gifts, then started the slow walk down the steps into the subway. As I entered the tunnel, a horrible feeling fell over me. I had no money. Nothing. Not even a quarter to give the man inside the booth for the subway token. Here I was, a law school graduate, a moment of triumph just celebrated, and still, I had nothing in my pockets. That would still take time.

I had to get home, because I had to drive my cab that night. I remember the feeling of having to go to the booth and asking the toll taker to let me onto the subway. I had all these gifts, and I had no way to get home. The tollbooth clerk is one of those anonymous souls who unknowingly becomes part of a larger story by virtue of a simple act of kindness. If you're reading this and vaguely recall letting a young man walk through your turnstile and board a train toward a brighter future, I would like to say *thank you.*

After three years and countless ticks on the odometer, I left the chauffeuring business and got my first job out of law school, with the then-prominent accounting firm Arthur Anderson. But as much as I'm a long-term, stick-with-it kind of guy, this is one instance where I knew that sticking around was not the road to a happy future.

On one of my first assignments, they took me out to Columbus, Ohio for an audit. They told me at 4 o'clock that I was going. I flew out there, I worked until midnight and I didn't come back to New York until the next day— where they expected me to work around the clock. When I finally got home, Judy said, "This job is history."

Not long after, I got a job as a litigating attorney on Long Island, and the rest is, well, you know.

CHAPTER 16

THE MEDIUM & THE MESSAGE

There's no definitive roadmap you can simply pick up and follow for getting where you want to go in life. You can't hop in a cab and ask the driver to take you there. Waze isn't going to cut it. Not as a real estate investor, not as a lawyer, an accountant, a teacher, a journalist, a chef, a sherpa… not as anything, actually. You make your own path with each step you take. You have to have a destination in mind, of course, set goals and create a plan that you intend to follow in order to reach them. You must have the conviction that the course you're laying out is the right one for you. You must believe.

But the route is going to more circuitous than direct in all likelihood. There will be sidesteps and off ramps and hazards and detours, and keeping that destination in mind amidst all that requires the same kind of focus and patience as real estate investing. It also takes the confidence to go down paths less traveled. Nobody knows what's down those roads—which is precisely why I've always taken them.

I believe in the power of reaching an audience in any way possible. In the early 1980s, when I'd been practicing law for a decade, the largest audience you could find was sitting in front of a television set. Remember, there was no internet, no YouTube, no social media.

I decided that the best way to promote myself and raise my profile was a TV show. People would see me and get to know me, and I thought eventually they would consider me their attorney.

Mind you, I'd never been a TV host before. But so what? I hadn't been a lawyer before becoming a lawyer, and that was working out pretty well. My idea was a relatively simple one: communicate, educate, illuminate. I'd go on TV and share my knowledge with a live call-in audience. As time went on, I would invite the top legal minds in New York to join my show to address questions I thought the public might want to ask.

Normally such face-to-face access with New York's legal luminaries would cost a person hundreds upon hundreds of dollars an hour, if you could get in front of them at all. This way was free, the advice and information on topics ranging from real estate issues, such as landlord-tenant problems or the difference between a condo and a co-op, to matrimonial laws and divorces to criminal law to whatever else might be engaging to the public and the legal community.

So with Judy producing and me on camera, *Lawline* hit the air in 1983 on cable access in New York City. Cable TV was in its relative infancy at that point, and most of

America didn't yet know how desperately they wanted their MTV. I didn't get cable at my Brooklyn apartment in those early years, and since the show was live (it went to tape later on), I didn't even get to watch myself! Plenty of others didn't, either, in the beginning.

Who would have dreamed it would become the longest-running legal TV show in history?

Over its 30-year run—eventually moving to PBS and garnering an audience not just in Manhattan but also upstate New York, Long Island, New Jersey and Connecticut—*Lawline* landed me the nickname "The Larry King of Law." The show became must-see TV for the legal set, and we drew the biggest names in the New York legal world—attorneys general, judges, top lawyers—to the chair across from me.

Although the e-cards probably haven't been jamming up your inbox, Law Day has been celebrated on May 1 in the United States since the Eisenhower Administration and *Lawline* was always part of the party. Every year, the Chief Judges of the State of New York would visit the show in recognition of, as the National Bar Association phrases it, this "national day set aside to celebrate the rule of law. Law Day underscores how law and the legal process have contributed to the freedoms that all Americans share." Those interviews remain among my favorites, both for fulfilling the show's mission to educate the masses and from a personal standpoint of being able to learn from the era's top legal minds.

There are too many to list, but a few spring to mind immediately. Chief Judge Jonathan Lippman was a wonderful, intelligent individual. He was for the law and for helping people—truly an amazing person. We had Judith Kaye, the only woman Chief Judge at the time. She was the first woman to be an Associate Justice on the New York State Court of Appeals, and I remember her saying at that time, "I'm the only judge on the court of appeals in history who ever wore red shoes!"

One of my favorite guests was Chief Judge Sol Wachtler— such an eloquent, exceptional and charming individual. Wachtler was a great legal mind with gubernatorial aspirations, but you may recall his name from the shocking arrest in 1992 and ultimate sentencing to 15 months in federal prison for threatening to kidnap the daughter of his former lover. But that's a tale for another time. (If you're interested, when you put down *I Can, I Will, I Must*, you can go pick up Wachtler's own book, *After the Madness*.)

Democrat, Republican, rowdy, reserved, *Lawline* invited and welcomed them all. We wanted a diversity of opinion, a range of personalities—that's the way to keep discussions lively and engaging. I even got the last interview with civil rights leader William Kunsler, who famously represented the Chicago Seven, before Kunsler died in 1995.

What I didn't get, at least not immediately, was clients—it took about four years before *Lawline* brought me any direct business. But by that point I would have kept going just for the fun of it, for the weekly adventure it provided, for the chance to enter people's living rooms and share my love of the law.

In addition to the weekly TV show, I'd been lecturing colleagues for years as part of the bar association's continuing legal education series. By now it was the late 1990s, and a little thing called the Internet Bubble was rapidly expanding. Everybody who wanted to be anybody was launching a dot-com. It was a crazy cocktail of the Wild West, the gold rush and a Wall Street bacchanalia the likes of which we'd never seen.

Aside from the fortunes being made, there was revolution in the air. Everything from retail commerce to dating to entertainment to education was being reevaluated. There were ways to reach people, to connect with them, that previously hadn't been possible.

I thought, "My gosh! This is the best thing since sliced bread!" I couldn't believe it. I was giving a lot of lectures at the time, and it struck me: I can give lectures to lawyers on the internet, and they can watch them at their leisure. Mind you, at the time no one had ever seen a smartphone yet. There was no YouTube, no outlet for lawyers—or anyone else, for that matter—to watch videos as a means of coursework. It was clear that we could change the very foundation of the continuing education model.

In 1999, the same year that the term "e-learning" was coined, I became the first continuing legal education provider to go online in New York State—no small feat, as New York is the biggest legal market in the country, if not the world. I spent a lot of money on the technology, a tremendous amount, but I knew I was looking at the future.

And then the bubble burst.

All at once, businesses like Pets.com. Webvan, Geocities, etoys and Flooz were left smoldering in the rubble. Their spectacular rises and even more spectacular crashes would come to define the dark side of the era. Fear spread, stock prices of digital enterprises plummeted, and, as hard as it may be to believe, there was a not-so-small contingency chirping that they now had proof to support the notion that this internet thing was just a fad.

Some of these people were in my orbit. They said I was nuts if I kept Lawline.com going, that I was throwing time and money into a dark, ever-deepening hole. *Shut it down* came the cries. *Shut it down. You're crazy if you keep this thing going.*

What was crazy, I believed, would be to ignore the gut

instinct telling me that a piece of a very exciting future was within my grasp. I was still a practicing attorney—Lawline.com was not my primary focus, but I maintained it year after year. By the time 2006 rolled around, the site still had a dozen or so courses that people were paying to watch every month. The tide was turning. Lawline.com just needed a champion, someone who saw the potential and could create a plan for its evolution—and execute it. Fortunately, I didn't have to look far.

Six years after the internet bubble burst, my son, David, graduated law school, presented my partner Ben Zalman and I with a visionary plan to redefine Lawline.com, and took over the company. David's pre–law school experience with a number of digital companies such as 24/7 Media—and perhaps a bit of his father's optimism and entrepreneurial spirit—has been invaluable. Shortly thereafter, my daughter, Michele, an American University Law School graduate, joined Lawline.com, and they've never looked back. Michele has been an integral part of Lawline.com's success, and brother and sister together make up the A-Team. One of my favorite expressions is "Teamwork Makes the Dream Work," and David and Michele embody that to its fullest.

Today, Lawline.com is the number one provider of continuing legal education (CLE) in the United States, with more than 125,000 attorney subscribers upwards of 3 million courses completed each year, and a library topping 1,500 lectures. The company has signed deals with prestigious law schools and been honored by the National Law Journal as one of the Top Online CLE Providers.

Lawline.com has 1,200 attorneys giving lectures, and at the end of 2018 we started exploring the possibility of opening the inventory up to the public. Hopefully we'll progress from the market of 1.2 million lawyers to a world of 7 billion people. If we do, I can't wait to see what happens next. It all almost leaves me speechless. Almost.

CHAPTER 17

SELLING YOURSELF

"Half the money I spend on advertising is wasted—the trouble is I don't know which half."

Entrepreneur John Wanamaker often gets credit for this business bon mot, which may speak more to his penchant for marketing and building a good story around himself than to the actual veracity of that attribution. He founded Wanamaker's, one of America's first department stores, in Philadelphia in the late 1800s, and grew the business and his brand through consistent advertising and promotion. His stores set themselves apart with things like sales— unheard of at the time—and price guarantees, all of it pushed into the public consciousness by the first full-page ads in local papers and another anomaly in that day and age: a professional copywriter.

Despite how you or others may read into his words, the guy probably saw very little in advertising that did not, on some level, work. Yet Wanamaker's quote (we're willing to give him the credit) has been something of a Zen koan in the marketing world for more than a century. If you've ever wondered how effective advertising and marketing really are, if you've pondered which campaigns, commercials, push notifications and social media posts truly leave their mark and which ones fail, you're not alone.

I don't believe that any marketing or advertising tree falls in the woods without making a sound—no matter how big or microscopic. It's all effective, it's all good. But marketing has to be part of a plan. You can't do it haphazardly.

Bottom line: Do it. You're going to have to market yourself and your properties to be successful. Partners, lenders, tenants, brokers, buyers—you want to be familiar, or at least not unknown, to them all. And you never know where they'll find you, especially if they aren't actively looking.

And the strategy must include multiple advertising outlets. Print media and mailings—although it's the most expensive form, mailing is still effective—as well as radio advertising. Today, of course, Facebook, Twitter, Instagram, all the social media outlets are your launching pad. The internet is integral—it should be first and foremost.

And you have to have a solid Google Résumé. When somebody types in your name, they should see a laundry list of positive results. Because if somebody wants to know about you, if somebody is going to buy something, invariably they're going to Google it.

Yes, you're going to get Googled. Don't feel intimidated. It's a good thing. You have a story to tell—that is a certainty, so you need to get it out there. Of course, you need to figure out what that story is. If you're going to be successful in real estate, or any other field, you're going to have to market yourself with the vision you create and the goals you set.

When I became a real estate broker in 2012, you might assume that my history in the legal world would have helped a great deal. When I joined Saunders & Associates, you'd think that my track record as a developer of legendary Hamptons properties might give me a leg up. Think again.

When I first became a broker, no one other than those in the industry knew who I was. I'd been a lawyer for so many years. But because I had the wherewithal, I probably advertised as much if not more than most brokers in the Hamptons.

Real estate has been called the sport of the Hamptons, and brokers there—the big ones, at least, the ones with 8 and 9 figures in sales—advertise as if they're gunning to outdo the Super Bowl, World Series, Kentucky Derby and whatever UFC bout is going to smash the current pay-per-view record. They promote themselves as much as, if not more than the properties they're representing. It's a sea of full-color ads in glossy, shiny high-end magazines, sometimes spanning as many as 8 or 10 pages. They use photos of mansions and oceanfront vistas that would leave you breathless, but they also use photos of themselves in various poses and situations—some are suit-and-tie polished, some are on a tennis court or at the beach with a surfboard—and they use impressive sums of money and time to build their own personal brands.

When I came out of retirement and entered the broker game, I did it primarily because I love real estate. But I wasn't going to enter the fray without taking my best shot at becoming a player. In creating my new brand, every detail mattered. Hundreds of images were taken at photo shoots, and I ultimately went with a picture of me stepping confidently from a home that I sold for $15.5 million (the first property I sold, an achievement few brokers in the United States could claim, I am proud to say). I ran print and digital ads, and made sure that my story was compelling enough to generate editorial features and interviews. Even my car played a starring role. My license plate is not an exercise in vanity, but rather a genuine invitation: CallAlan.

People did, though not at first. In fact, the first year I didn't get one sale or one rental. But by the second year it started coming in, and I sold probably close to $100 million in real estate.

Stick to your plan, look for your opportunities, then go forward with conviction. It's okay to feel some fear, those tugs of apprehension, but it's not okay to wear them like weights around your ankles. Push through them. If I didn't persevere, I would not have made a name for myself in the highly competitive world of Hamptons brokers. If I let myself be governed by doubt, I never would have attempted a marketing play that helped catapult my law business years earlier.

In 1999, the FDA approved Merck & Co.'s nonsteroidal anti-inflammatory drug rofecoxib, which many said would change the lives of people suffering from arthritis and acute or chronic pain. You may recall it as Vioxx.

The drug was a massive hit. Within five years it had been used by more than 84 million people. In 2004, after studies showed an increased risk of heart problems associated with the drug, Merck announced it was pulling it from the market. When I heard the news, I saw an opportunity.

The day before the news would hit the mass media, I called the New York City radio station 1010 WINS—arguably the top all-news radio station in the country—and told them I wanted to buy spots the following day. I'd run ads for my firm, Zalman & Schnurman, with WINS in the past, and I knew the breadth and power of this station's reach. But this time when the ad sales rep on the line asked how many spots I wanted, I said simply, "I want them all."

To buy every single spot of available air time on a top station in Manhattan takes a small fortune, and that's exactly what I was willing to risk. I knew I had to have as many as I could get, and I knew it would work.

The ads started running the next morning, continuing throughout the day, telling anyone who'd used Vioxx to call Zalman & Schnurman. At first, our phones were quiet. Then came one call, and another, and soon they were ringing off the hook, so much so that we had to hire extra staff to handle the volume.

Regardless of your field, all advertising works, and you never ever know where a client or a sale comes from. Because it's all part of branding, no matter what you're selling.

You may not think you're getting any response at three o'clock in the morning when you're running a TV ad or a radio ad, but when you run it on an ongoing basis, you'd be amazed at the benefit it has.

Not every marketing effort needs to be wildly original or innovative, either. My firm once sent out 15,000 refrigerator magnets: "If you're in an accident, call ___." For years and years, we'd get calls, because there was a certain segment of the population that put these magnets on their refrigerator, and if they had an accident—or even if they had a friend or a relative who did—the number they had to call was ours.

Naturally, not everything I've tried has been a winner. Not every radio spot inspired thousands of phone calls, or even one. Not every press release fills convention rooms with rowdy crowds of reporters. There were print ads for homes that I thought would draw *oohs* and *aahs* but in the end sparked no interest. So I made tweaks, tinkered with photos, ad copy or the timing of a campaign. The point is, you have to keep trying.

Marketing is all testing. You have to see what works. And if it doesn't work, you try something else, and if that doesn't work, you try something else. You never know where that next sale is going to come from, so you have to try everything, and try it consistently, day in and day out. You have to be out there.

That means in person as well as virtually. Networking is crucial to your brand. What do I mean by networking? Well, social networking is important, so you'll put everyone you know into your LinkedIn database and make sure they're following you on whatever platform you choose. But if you have a product or you're selling yourself, you have to go to places to meet other people. Face-to-face.

Your local chamber of commerce likely hosts breakfasts, lunches, dinners, cocktail hours—go attend them all. Start up conversations with the owners or managers when you walk into a local business. Engage with people, share your story and allow others to share theirs with you. *Connect.*

Relationships and success are tied together. Meeting people, talking to people, speaking to groups—it's part of your branding. People want to trust you, they want you to be credible, they want to meet you. Never underestimate the potential of even one conversation. Just like I never underestimate the importance of a single sale, because that's how you build. One client at a time, one conversation at a time.

Now go Google "Alan Schnurman Bedbugs."

Wait, not right this minute. Later, when you've finished the book but can't get to that itch of curiosity that's just been planted.

What, you can't wait? You sure? Okay, just turn the page...

CHAPTER 18

WHEN THE BEDBUGS BITE

By this point, I'm assuming you've taken me up on the suggestion from the prior chapter and searched "Alan Schnurman Bedbugs." I'll take that assumption to its logical next step and assume that you'd like to know the story behind it.

Sitting in my New York City office on a day that hadn't yet stood out from any other, I took a call from a woman in Chicago that would change the course of my career. She'd been referred by someone I knew in California, and her tale was like nothing I'd ever heard.

The woman and her husband had taken a vacation to the Nevele—a historic hotel in what had been one of the crown jewels of the Catskill Mountains during its heyday in the '60s (yes, when I was working nearby) and '70s. At just over 100 years old by this time, the Nevele was something of a shadow of its former self, when it was bustling with families from Manhattan and hosting the likes of President Lyndon Johnson. But even its steady decline couldn't prepare this woman for the surprise guests she encountered.

Bedbugs.

Have you ever actually seen a bedbug? If you answer in the affirmative, then surely you've pondered why anyone would conjure their image and undermine the notion of sleeping tight with the suggestion of not letting these little creatures bite. But I digress.

She told me she'd been bitten and wanted to do something about it. I said to her, "Well, I don't really handle those types of cases." She said, "Well, I got bitten many, many times, and I have photos. Can I email them to you?"

I said, "Sure, but I'm telling you, I don't handle those types of cases."

The photos arrived. Bites all over her body, some 500 of them, most the size of quarters. The woman actually had a flask of the bedbugs, had kept them in a jar, and I got a video of that, too. The visuals were too much to ignore.

Great theater was afoot. Yes, there was a legitimate case at the heart, but bugs and bites and graphic images, well, that's the kind of stuff the media, and the general public, cannot resist. I alerted outlets far and wide that we would hold a press conference, and stoked the fire just a little by attaching a trio of photos of the woman along with the release. On the morning of the press conference, the library at my law firm was absolutely packed, an atmosphere not unlike you might find on a Hollywood junket. I knew that the bug photos had drawn the crowd, although filing a suit seeking $20 million certainly didn't hurt.

Every local TV station was there, the AP was there, every newspaper except *The New York Times* was there. Afterward, speaking to the guy from the AP who I knew very well, I said, "Boy, this is some news conference." He said, "Alan, you have no idea. By tomorrow, everybody in the world will know about this case."

The guy was right. Sure enough, the next morning the phone was ringing nonstop and the offers were pouring in. I got calls from the *Today* show, *Good Morning America* and CNN.

They all wanted my client, and they wanted me on the air with her. The *Today* show and *Good Morning America* both wanted the exclusive. And I thought, How could I give either of you the exclusive? I've got you both!

Well, *Good Morning America* said nope, we want the exclusive, and otherwise it won't happen. Well, I said, that's fine, I'll go on the *Today* show. It's my favorite show, to be quite frank. And they promised me Katie Couric on the couch.

So, *Good Morning America* said, "You know what we'll do? We'll pick you up in the morning, and we'll interview you, and we'll show it simultaneously with the *Today* show." After I taped *Good Morning America*, I went over to the *Today* show, which I happen to watch every morning.

It was a dream come true. I was sitting on the couch, and then who sits down? Matt Lauer! "Matt!" I said, "They promised me Katie!" But he interviewed my client and me, it was great, and then we went over to CNN and they did a whole segment there. It was quite a day.

The Nevele case wrapped up eventually and was resolved, but the bedbugs story became something like the Harry Potter saga. The stories kept coming—the same villain with different victims, all coming to me to wage battle. In 2007, a Fordham student enlisted my help after claiming her off-campus housing at an NYC hotel had exposed her to bedbugs. A few years after that, as the national frenzy over these critters was rising to a crescendo, a couple claimed that New York's famous Waldorf Astoria hotel had put them in a guest room with the pests. And to make matters worse, the bedbugs allegedly came home with them to Michigan. There are certainly better souvenirs from the Big Apple.

I didn't take every bedbug case that came my way, but I made the most of the ones I took.

Full disclosure: Books and words are great. Whether you're reading this on your phone or a tablet, listening to the audio version or holding a printed copy in your hands, we know you have an affinity for them. But there are certain things the internet can deliver that simply don't come across in all their glory unless you look them up online.

Bedbugs, for instance.

Go ahead, you know you want to. I'll be here when you get back.

CHAPTER 19

LOVE WHAT YOU'RE DOING, OR A PORTRAIT OF THE ARTIST

In the early 2010s, the real estate market in the Hamptons was starting its slow, steady climb back toward the loftier latitudes it had inhabited prior to 2008. At the time, I was the new kid on the block in my fledgling career as a broker.

One Sunday, another broker comes to one of my open houses and says, "Alan, let me ask you a question. I know you as a developer, for years, and you developed major projects—why do you want to be a broker?"

I laughed and I didn't say much in response, but I thought, *Why do I want to be a broker?* I love this! Are you kidding? This is so much fun!

There you have it. You're getting into the world of real estate investing—or whatever professional path you're choosing—to make money, to improve your financial situation. But you should also be doing it because there's something there that you love. I didn't need a job when I joined Saunders & Associates in Bridgehampton. I didn't need to be driving all over the Hamptons showing houses to prospective buyers, or dealing with demanding sellers who expected me to deliver full-asking-price-paying clients and maybe even a basket of croissants to their door (the

Hamptons is a demanding market, after all).

What I *did* need to do, what we *all* need to do, is fulfill an inner need, find a challenge and figure out a way to rise up and meet it. It's hard work for a person to realize how good they really are. Who amongst us really appreciates how good we really are? Depending on how we were raised, we feel there's somebody better, somebody who knows more—there's always a better writer, a better lawyer, a better real estate broker. But the truth is, you have to realize how good you really are.

Real estate has always spoken to me as an investor, but through my years as a developer I discovered that it could provide an outlet for other passions and talents I possess. Because real estate is creative.

I'm not an artist, a sculptor or a musical talent. That said, buying a piece of land, hiring an architect, working with a builder, an interior decorator, a site planner, a surveyor, a land expert to figure out the best possible use of a particular property—it's all part of a creative process.

That may not be obvious to you as you drive past homes, even office buildings and public spaces. But step back and look deeper. Consider the details, the intricacies in planning and execution that go into every phase of raising a structure from the imagined to the real.

The whole process of building a house or developing land requires vision from the outset. To say you build from the ground up might seem obvious. But just two paragraphs ago it wasn't obvious that you were about to wade into the world of an artist, maybe even take your first steps toward becoming one yourself. Sometimes, you have to start at the bottom. And the land and the location are the most important part of the process.

You should bring your architect to the land long before you submit an offer, and you should be armed with questions. How would you situate the house to take advantage of the beautiful vistas? Which way should the house face? Would you align it straight on the lot? At an angle? Next you speak to your landscape architect: If the house is built on the lot at this angle, how would you landscape the grounds? These questions are critical. Remember, this is your project—your vision coming to life.

Now, keep in mind, and I say this in all modesty, I have no original thoughts. If you're looking for someone who's a genius, you have to go somewhere else. But I'll tell you what: I can spot great work, and I can copy.

One day you'll choose a location where you'll start your own development project, and it will have its own personality and inspiration, to be sure. On the East End of Long Island, where architectural legends such as Stanford White, Charles Gwathmey and Norman Jaffe have left their mark in monuments of wood and steel and glass—where modern architects and designers have taken up the mantle and concocted creations for the most discerning clients and homeowners—there's plenty of originality from which to borrow.

For years I've traveled the Hamptons and picked up what I consider the best of its architecture: a sloping roof, a jaw-dropping kitchen, a luxurious bath, a unique door placement. I've had no educational background in this, but I have a lot of experience. Being a real estate broker helps immensely because I know what people want. It's the expansive home theater, a wonderful children's playroom, a gym, a wine cellar, a billiard room—in short, everything they don't have in Manhattan. When you sit down with the architect, these are all things up for discussion. Even though the architect does his or her work, it's ultimately your responsibility—you're in charge of the project.

At this stage, you're now an artist, but so is your architect. And if the architect wants to do something that doesn't fit your vision, that you fear won't mesh with your potential buyers' desires, you must remember that you as the developer must sell it. You never want to be too "out there."

I like to be in the mid-range. I don't want to be too far afield of what will appeal to the middle range of the market. I'm not talking about list price, mind you, but rather what's in fashion for the public at this particular time.

Couture and prêt-á-porter aren't just for what's hanging in your closet. Yes, architecture is about fashion just like clothing. Sometimes modern is in; flat-roof houses with floor-to-ceiling windows. Other times it's cottage-style houses of the early 19th and 20th centuries. Back and forth the pendulum swings, so you have to make sure that the architecture you're employing will be in fashion when you need it to be. You can't know the future, but it's your job to at least glimpse where it might go.

If you're building a home, it isn't going to be ready for one and a half or two years, so you have to anticipate what fashion will be desired. Then you have to sit down with your builder. What materials will be used? What's the budget? Once the architect has drawn the plans, can it actually be done?

Then I hire an interior designer, who picks out my finishes. Sometimes white floors are in, other times dark hardwoods, sometimes tile. Years ago we used marble, then granite, and now glass countertops are very much in favor.

Architect, landscape architect, builder—and you're not done yet. Land surveyors, inspectors, painters, electricians, the list goes on and on. It's a collaborative effort, and everybody has to be coordinated. Everything has to be planned.

This is a team process and you're the owner, GM and coach, all rolled into one. It's an orchestra and you're the conductor, as well as the person who has to make sure all the seats in the concert hall are filled. Pick your metaphor.

I can't build a house, I can't knock a nail, but I'm the one who writes the check. It's my neck on the line, and if I can't sell a house, it falls on me. You want a product that the market wants, that the market will buy and the market will absorb.

And it just so happens that I have one in mind. Come step inside...

CHAPTER 20

BREATHTAKING SAGAPONACK

Every home in the Hamptons tells a story. It might whisper of agrarian roots from centuries past or shout of newfound success. It may have been passed down through generations or be as new as this morning's sunrise. For each home there's a tale to be told—you just have to listen.

Up on the roof deck of the house known as Breathtaking Sagaponack, the tale of the final home to rise on one of the more renowned pieces of land on Long Island's East End begins with a glance east, at the waves breaking on the Atlantic, starting the stir of salt air.

Incorporated in 2005, the village has a history stretching back to the mid 1600s, through centuries of potato farming and real estate that transformed those fields into hedgerow-lined parcels owned by some of the wealthiest and most well-known people on the planet. Its population now hovers right around 300, give or take, and there's still a one-room schoolhouse for children in kindergarten through third grade, all snuggled into the 4.7 square miles that make up this slice of Hamptons heaven.

The name Sagaponack is derived from the local Native American word *Sagg*, meaning "place where the large ground-nuts grow," but it may as well translate to "Place

Where You Find the Most Expensive Zip Code in America." This was in fact a distinction bestowed upon the famous 11962 and its chart-topping $5.125 million median home value, a village that has hosted the likes of music legend Billy Joel, actor Roy Scheider, *Tonight Show* host Jimmy Fallon and renowned author Truman Capote. Financier Ira Rennert—with his 100,000-square-foot compound—and any number of Wall Street titans could have homes anywhere in the world, and yet somehow they landed here.

Amid the wealth and wow factor surrounding the place, one can't overlook the natural wonders that make Sagaponack such an enviable location for developers and homeowners alike. The vistas and ocean breezes are, in a word, spectacular.

Home, said T.S. Eliot, is where one starts from, and the start of the home I named Breathtaking Sagaponack goes back earlier than the pouring of the foundation, before the blueprints were drawn up, even before I had any idea I'd be building here at all.

The story begins back in 2005 when my partners and I purchased 26 acres in Bridgehampton. In my 20 years of investing in real estate up until that point, I'd never bought land to develop. But I knew this lot on Ocean Road just north of Bridge Lane was a fantastic location, and for $12 million we entered the world of Hamptons developers.

As if fate had been waiting for me to dip my toes in these waters, it delivered a tidal wave. While I was going through the approval process to develop the land known as the Ocean Highland project, another 42 acres came up in Sagaponack, and I knew exactly what to do. I had my team in place—my lawyers, environmental specialists, surveyors—and I knew that no one should own it but me.

This time would be a bit tougher. With such prime real estate at stake, there were several interested parties. There was a bid of $28 million for the 42 acres, and since I bid $25 million, I didn't get it. I'd moved on to looking at other projects when I got a call from the seller's lawyer, who asked if I could close within 30 days. I said yes.

I had to raise the money—which quite frankly was a challenge, because I still owned the 26 acres in Bridgehampton—but I was confident I could do it. The seller's lawyer sent over a contract for $28 million, which I changed to $25 million and returned with a deposit of $2.5 million. The next day I received the signed contract and we had a deal.

Now all I had to do was get the rest of the money. In one month.

I had what's called a time of the essence clause, and I signed the contract on June 1, put down $2.5 million from my partners and me, and then had to raise enough equity.

The bank was going to give me a $15 million loan—the same bank that gave me the money to finance Ocean Highland. Remember, I hadn't sold Ocean Highland yet, but Sagaponack was so hot at the time, I knew it was an opportunity I couldn't pass up.

Days went by. Then weeks. And the money simply was not there. With only seven days left until the deadline, I was still $1.5 million short. I couldn't eat—every day I was losing weight, I was down to 138 pounds. I couldn't sleep. Seven days. Six days. Five days. I had $2.5 million of my and my partners' money under contract, and had I not been able to close, I would have lost it all. Then, out of the blue, my architect said, "Let me put you together with these people who've heard of you," and the next thing I knew they wired me $1.5 million. These were people I'd never met—they only knew my reputation. And I was able to close.

The Ocean Highland approvals still hadn't come through at the time, so now I was sitting on more than 65 acres of ultra-prime Hamptons real estate. Stress and gut-twisting stomachaches aside, having both parcels put me in a rarefied air: my partners and I were one of the largest owners of developable land in Sagaponack and Bridgehampton, south of the highway.

The distinction didn't last long, which was, of course, the intent. After 30 months, we finally got approvals for the

Bridgehampton parcel. We had subdivided the 26 acres into six separate lots, though the Southampton Town board gave us a scare, narrowly green-lighting the project by a single vote. As we debated how to price the lots, a big deal went down in nearby East Hampton, where a Wall Street tycoon purchased something like 100 acres—and a number of houses he planned to demolish—for $100 million. I figured, well, if he paid $100 million for that, I'll price mine at $37.5 million. And sure enough, somebody came up to the plate and met my price.

As for the 42 acres of the Sagaponack Daniel Hedges deal, that took 10 years to become an overnight success. The speed of the sale for that $25 million lot lies in stark contrast to the time it took to actually develop the land. There are zoning rights, development rights, demolition rights—there are often old buildings on these centuries-old family farms in the Hamptons. We even had to find a new location for a 1930s foursquare farmhouse that was on the property. It was eventually picked up and moved to a nearby expanse of land, but not until battles among local residents, politicians and even land preservation groups had been waged.

Unfortunately, when I got my approvals, the Great Recession hit. But I had some of the most desirable land in the United States—Sagaponack, south of the highway—and I sold all my lots. Nobody else sold. I lowered my prices, I lowered my margins, and I moved them. But the last lot, I decided to keep it and build on it—that's the start of Breathtaking Sagaponack.

Holding onto that last piece of the historic property was a dream realized, where I played the role of developer, owner and broker, not to mention visionary. Working with architect Val Florio, contractor Fountainhead Construction and interior designer Christy Hanson, we created a masterpiece.

Many of my decisions about the scope and details of the build were informed by listening to the desires expressed by visitors to my open houses when I was representing other listings as a broker. From the elevator to the glass-enclosed breezeway, the two laundry rooms to the six fireplaces, the main-floor coat closet (which some have said could double as the Yankees locker room) to the butler's pantry, I knew what the high-end market wanted. Over and over I had heard, "If the house only had this or that…" So I tried to deliver everything the Hamptons market desired.

First and foremost, that translated to a large, open concept first floor, flowing from the entranceway to the kitchen, then the family room to the living room. The kitchen has countertops of Imperial Danby marble and room for 14 to dine in view of the 26-acre reserve abutting the nearly two-acre lot. The junior master has a covered outside terrace and fireplace (the house has six fireplaces in all).

Throughout there are subtle touches, such as you'll see glancing up to the dining room ceiling, adorned with a circle of woodwork lined with lights surrounding actual silver leaf that can be hard to identify depending upon the light of the day. It could be silver or gold, or some precious metal mined only here on the East End.

Up one set of stairs is a private guest wing with its own living room, a terrace overlooking the reserve and the grounds, two bedrooms and two baths. It's a private, self-contained unit—almost like having a guesthouse. Up another set of stairs you'll encounter the double-door entry master bedroom, with its fireplace, massive terrace, and bath with not just a marble shower, but its own terrace as well.

Everything is soft, simple. The whole house is greys, off-greys and whites. When it was designed, the market was a little different than that of even a few years earlier—people want traditional on the outside and modern on the inside. Keep in mind, the market for these houses is young people in their 30s and 40s with two or three children, quite successful in their professional life, and they want a full entertainment environment. The Hamptons is no longer just a summer getaway—it's now a year-round playground.

The lower level embraces that notion. There's a movie theater with a 13-foot screen, and a glass-enclosed wine cellar with stainless steel racks and room for a table to dine in the midst of an oenophile's treasures. A wood-paneled billiards room, a rec room with a gas fireplace, a service kitchen and a gym that would make L.A. Fitness envious round out the amenities. Outside I built a below-grade garden, so this huge gym looks out on a beautiful garden with trees and flowers.

The outside of the home is as much a part of its soul as the interior. Pulling up, one's welcoming impression is a covered porch, a nod to my own past. When I was a kid my mother was always working, and she would send me away to camp. One of my favorite things about camp was sitting on the porch and watching the rain. So I have a sweet spot for covered porches—they protect you from the sun and the rain, and yet you can still enjoy the elements.

Out back is a gunite saltwater swimming pool, 72 feet long and 18 feet wide with a spa, adjacent to a long pagoda and pool house, and enough bluestone hardscape for a party of 300 people (the outdoor kitchen and full kitchen in the pool house will keep food and drinks flowing). An expanse of grass large enough for a baseball game beckons, although home runs may soar onto the Har-Tru tennis court, sunken just alongside the reserve to seamlessly blend in with the picturesque, quiet, sincere vistas.

Sincere. That one word, more than any other, was my charge in creating Breathtaking Sagaponack, the perfect coda to this story that started on those acres of land more than a decade earlier. You might think it would be hard for me to see this chapter end. But as I said early on, experience comes in the journey, not the destination, and I know that the buyers will create their own story.

In all, the house took two years to build, and one of the reasons is that it was all done by onsite craftsmen. It just takes time to create a masterpiece. I can't paint a painting, I can't play an instrument, but building a house—buying the land, dealing with the architect, the contractors, the interior designer—is my creative outlet. This house is a piece of art.

Two months post-completion, it sold for $18.1 million.

CHAPTER 21

PICKING YOUR PARTNERS

Breathtaking Sagaponack was a labor of love, but a labor nonetheless—and that's before a shovel went in the ground or a hammer hit a nail. From the very start, nearly a decade earlier, I couldn't have done it by myself. That's not because I wasn't used to flying solo. Far from it. In fact, it was the experience I'd gained over many years that made it possible to pull together the team to make such a development deal possible.

Before I went through that process, I always invested on my own. I started small. My wife and I lived significantly under our means. We started buying condos, and then after that I bought mixed-use buildings with my partner Ben Zalman. Ben and I have been together 45 years, and we still share in many properties to this day.

Early on, I put up the money for my real estate investments on my own, but over time the desire to undertake larger deals required larger financial resources. How do you know when it's time to elevate your game? It's a matter of crunching your numbers, seeing how much money you have, always having money in the bank. If you're short on cash for a project, you call on your friends and your relatives. That's how I did it.

Picking your partners is a nuanced process. One qualification, naturally, is that they have the money. But there's more than that. A partner should be Credible, Reliable, Ethical, Experienced and Trustworthy. CREET. Truly knowing these people, their personalities, their demeanors, their risk tolerance, their willingness to commit to someone else's plan and see it through to its end. I pick my partners very, very carefully. You have to be careful, because a bad partner, like a bad marriage, can be very challenging.

When I bought two lots in Sagaponack, I brought in friends I'd known forever—lawyer friends, college friends, some going back as far back as high school. I was clear about what I wanted to do, how I was going to do it, and what the expectations were.

We bought the property for $950,000, built a house for approximately $1.4 million and sold it for $4.3 million, right after 9/11. It was pond-front with an ocean view. Today that house is probably worth almost $10 million.

We did quite well, and we did a second and third deal, and we kept doing well. But in the back of my mind I also knew that no market goes only in one direction. I had faith in my partners, and vice versa, but I was concerned that when the market turned, I would have challenges with my investors.

Sure enough, the market did turn. You probably remember

those years—and not fondly. The cracks in the dam began showing around 2007, and the flood finally crashed through in 2008. The country struggled to keep its collective head above the rising waters of a financial crisis the likes of which hadn't been seen since the Great Depression.

Nothing was selling. Everything was flat, if not depreciating. The stock market was going down every day, commodities were going down, bonds were challenged. At one point, nobody was investing in anything. People weren't even buying cars or washing machines. People who had their life savings in the market were depressed, and they started selling.

Real estate was no exception to this new way of life. Even in the Hamptons, the market had been hit hard. And yet, of all my investors, not one called me up to say they were unhappy. *Not one.* I was honestly shocked. Our group owned a good deal of Hamptons land at that point. We'd put $25 million into the big Sagaponack deal in 2005, and had eight lots and a reserve to sell...and they weren't moving.

Put yourself back in those days for a moment. There was panic sweeping the country. You'd meet people at the ATM or, more incredibly, waiting on line to see a teller face-to-face, just to check that their money was still in the bank. Retirement funds were shrinking away to nothing.

Foreclosures piled up by the hour. *Bailout* and *burst bubble* were the terms on everyone's lips. Only now, after years of financial healing, can we look back and see the Great Recession as any less of the economic nightmare than it really was.

And still, not one phone call from a partner.

But what I did—because I respect my investors' money more than my own—was lower the prices. The original plan was to get $8.5 million for each of those lots, some a bit more or less than others. But dropping them to $5 million proved to be a magic formula at a time when many felt all hope was lost and not even supernatural powers could get things moving again.

And in the worst market I've ever been in, I was able to sell most of my lots—at a profit. Not as much as Ocean Highland, not as much as we thought we were going to make, but everyone was grateful they had money coming in when they weren't seeing returns from other investments.

My banker, who was in Kansas City, told me I was the only land guy in America that he financed who was actually paying him back. Of course, Sagaponack was the best land in America, because even in bad times, wealthy people are still wealthy. Their net worth may drop by millions upon millions, but they're still wealthy, and they still understand a value buy.

Now, nobody has a perfect track record. Not everyone has stuck with me every time. My partners and I once had an office building in Manhattan, and one investor wanted to be bought out because we had been holding it so long. One of the other investors bought him out, and unfortunately for that one investor, the property is now worth almost twice what we paid for it.

In this particular case, when I say long term, we're talking about almost a decade. That might seem like a very long time to wait. But if those were the expectations from the start, and you're signing on for such a deal or you're asking partners to join you on such a long journey, the length of time can't be taken lightly. If you get on a plane from New York City to Tahiti and you're told it's going to take 13 hours to reach paradise, don't buckle up and think to yourself that you could be at Bali Hai in 6.

That's why I emphasize that your expectations should always be for the long term. That particular investor worked with me just that one time. He was bought out at what he invested, so he got all his money back, but if he'd stuck it out he would have done exceptionally well. Although it's worth substantially more than we paid for it, we're actually getting much more, because it's a leveraged deal, so we only put down 25%.

The idea of buying and holding for the long term means you're going to be in business with these people for years, which is another key reason I started off with friends and family as partners. (Of course, they're incredibly nice people.) Now, there's an adage out there somewhere warning about issues of money and business and family and friends, but if you have a plan—and that's where all that research and due diligence comes in—and you transparently lay that plan out to your partners, no matter who they are, the odds are strongly in your favor.

I've worked with my family my whole life. Judy and I worked together, my children work on the internet company. But everyone has to be flexible, and everyone has to keep in mind it's family first, business second. Try to take emotion out of it, try to remove the fact that you used to beat each other up when you were in high school. No matter what happens, family is the center of your universe—and everything else is background.

Whether it's family and friends or outsiders you're bringing into your inner circle, managing expectations and making sure everyone's on the same page is at the top of your priority list. It's up to you to make sure that everyone has the same goals in a deal. Success begins with strong, clear communication to your partners about every aspect of the project. You must, from the very start, reinforce the notion that this isn't an overnight flip-and-get-rich plan. Don't be shy about it. Put that fact out there for everyone to see.

You really have to write out your goals and expectations on

paper—for example, we're going to hold a property for 10 years and we expect such and such a growth rate. That's critical. Everybody knows what to expect, there's a written agreement, shared goals. Nothing will sour a deal like unrealistic expectations.

Keep in mind that these are only expectations subject to market conditions that can substantially alter the profits and the time you place the property on the market. That reservation should always be discussed, and if the goals are written down, so must this reservation.

There will be forces fighting you in this arena, no doubt, especially at the outset. You've seen those TV shows where some couple buys a house, fixes it up and flips it for a six-figure profit in two weeks? Those shows aren't going to help. Your research and in-depth understanding of your market and particular project are essential, but so is your ability to stress that anybody joining you as a partner simply cannot be in it for the quick buck.

In real estate everybody knows location, location, location. But right after location, location, location comes patience, patience, patience. Real estate is slow, it's reliable, it's methodical—and if you have the patience and a good location, you can be financially secure.

CHAPTER 22

TOO MUCH OF A GOOD THING IS NOT A GOOD THING

A guys walks into a bank and asks for $10 million...

Sounds like the start of a bad joke, right? It very well could be, if the punch line is the bank's telling the guy he isn't getting the money because he didn't know how to go about asking.

But it doesn't have to have a bitter ending at all. It could also be the start of a tale about a historic real estate investment, a never-before-attempted deal. It could be your own story, even.

Remember way back in "When Is a Good Time to Buy," I told you that money and financing were the last things you were going to think about. You were going to learn a market, do your due diligence and embrace the ideas of patience and confidence and optimism.

You've done all that, or at least you've learned how. Now, let's talk about the money.

Every project has costs that go far beyond the asking price of the property. There are closing costs, title fees, appraisal fees. There's the surveyor, the land expert, the pest inspection, your attorney, interest and amortization on the mortgage. Depending on the particulars of the project, the list will grow and shrink. You're going to need money during the acquisition period, then again during the construction or renovation period, when you're going to be making improvements and adding value.

In any real estate purchase, there are two things you'll focus on. First, will the project appreciate over a long period of time? Second, do I want to add value to the project as soon as I buy it? Usually, if things go as planned, not only do you receive the value of the original outlay and your renovation, but you've increased the entire value of the project well beyond the original purchase price.

If you borrow money for any of these undertakings, there comes a point where you have to pay it back. This might seem obvious, but it bears repeating because it isn't easy to get that money from a bank in the first place.

Remember, banks are in the business of lending money, but they're not in the business of losing money, so you have to show them that yours will be a viable project.

Unlike the gentleman who started off this chapter, missing perhaps only a rabbi and a priest to have elevated himself to a higher station in life, you won't be strolling into the bank and simply asking for a mountain of money. You're going to run your numbers to make sure you understand all the costs, both to acquire a property and then improve it, maintain it and carry it along. And you're going to understand leverage.

Simply put, leverage means how much you borrow in relation to how much a property is worth. Taking a loan to finance a property can be a good thing, since it will allow you to buy more than you could with just the cash you have on hand.

Leverage can bring with it tremendous risk. Not the kind of risks we've been talking about—the ones you take because you've calculated them from every angle. The risk that comes with too much leverage can ruin your chances of success quickly and utterly.

How? Why? Because as I've said, real estate, besides location, takes patience. Real estate takes time. And if you're not patient, bad things can happen. A market can turn against you.

That's not going to be pretty. Too much of a good thing is, usually, too much.

Let's say you take on a large mortgage to buy a property because you're convinced you can, for example, fix it up in short order and turn it into a place somebody else will buy from you quickly and at a profit. The amount of money the bank was willing to lend you made it impossible for you to say no. And you hardly had to put your own money up at all. You even got a second mortgage on the property.

Then, factors beyond your control start to rear their ugly head and the market goes through a consolidation. You're stuck. Nobody wants to buy or even rent the property now, at least not at a price that will cover your costs—to say nothing of those gains that are now part of some dream, it seems, that's fading further and further out of memory. Your cash reserves are dwindling, because you still have those high payments that must go to the bank on a regular basis.

Say you get a 75% mortgage and then a 20% second mortgage and you're into it for only 5% and the market turns against you. How are you going to pay all those mortgages? How are you going to be patient? How are you going to let the market go down for two or three years, how are you going to sustain that? You're not. You're going to give it back to the bank.

This part of the story always seems to end up on the cutting room floor when they put together those flip-it-and-make-money-overnight shows. I'm not a flipper. I have flipped properties, but only because I bought them at the right time and got an offer I couldn't turn down. But I've never set out to flip a property right away. Never. Because it's a program for failure—and I don't like to lose. If I can't hold something for 10 years, I don't buy it.

When it comes to investing, nothing is haphazard, no stone is left unturned. From the first internet search on a property to your first offer, you'll see why tracking all those details is vital. Those written plans and notes we talked about earlier were not some minor exercise. Not only did they help you arrive at the project for which you're now seeking funding, but they'll help you get that very funding itself.

When it's time to go to the bank, I create what I call my playbook. Think Bill Belchick heading into the Super Bowl. The playbook discusses everything about the project, and will serve as both a textbook and a blueprint. Remember, you're going to meet with the bank in order to educate them about your investment project at every level. Think of it as a boardroom presentation, a job interview and a small college lecture rolled into one.

First, I'm assuming the bank knows nothing about the area where I'm looking to invest, so I discuss the location. I try to include any other kind of literature about the location that I can get off the internet. I include a map so they can get the area's aerial perspective, whether it's the Hamptons or New York City or Brooklyn, and I point out other places of vibrancy on the map—this building just sold for such and such, for example. I'll put number 1, number 2, number 3 and so on. And then later on in my playbook, I'll actually discuss what number 1 sold for, and then what it rented for—let's assume it was a multiple dwelling of 50 units, and the average rent was $50 per square foot per year—then I back that up, and I do that with three or four different comps.

Even if you're experienced, the bank may not just take *your* word for it. This is a risk on their part too, you know. The more support you can get from respected sources to back up your numbers and facts, the stronger your case will be. For example, I'll typically get a letter from a local broker showing what similar buildings have sold and rented for in the area. I'll include letters from a surveyor, an architect, a land planner. A compelling photo gallery is a must. Everything is strategically packaged to create the most compelling story possible.

I like to do all their work for them. Then I do a whole summary of the managing partners. I go into their backgrounds, what kind of real estate they've done in the past, what types of projects they've worked on and the success rate of those projects. This background is part of the story because the sole fact that the partners are kicking in money may not be enough. Their history as a team demonstrates that the group can do this project because they've done it before.

Now, if you're a first-timer, and your partners are first-timers, don't be discouraged. You must remember the lessons of "Selling Yourself"—you have a story to tell.

You're talking about your background, your education, all the research you've done on the area. But then you really need what every successful person has: perseverance.

I compare it to people in the entertainment industry. The people who you see on TV, in the movies, on Broadway, they tried year after year and were turned down. They were too tall, they were too short, I'm looking for a brunette and you're a blonde. There were so many times that they didn't get the job. And you may be turned down by the first 20 institutions. But that 21st institution—that's the one, and that's how you start.

How you finish is up to you.

CHAPTER 23

ATTITUDE EQUALS ALTITUDE

Tenzing-Hillary Airport has been called the most dangerous airport in the world, claiming the lives of more than 20 people since 2004 amid myriad crashes and other accidents. At 9,100 feet it's the highest-altitude airport on earth, and its one and only runway is 1,500 feet long, ending in an immovable mountainside for incoming planes.

When I decided to set foot on Mount Everest, landing here was where the journey would have to begin. The exhausting 30 hours of flights and stopovers from New York to London, London to Bahrain, Bahrain to Katmandu was not going to deter me. Stories about the unpleasant fate of other fliers was not going to stop me, either.

Attitude is one of the most important things. There are certain people who always have a poor attitude, who are always looking at the glass as half empty. In order to not get caught up in negativity, you have to work on your attitude every day. That's why I have my sayings—it's not nonchalant. Attitude equals altitude. Always try to have a good attitude—even if a mountain is rushing toward you at hundreds of miles per hour while you sit in a plane descending on an airport so dangerous that only eight pilots on the planet are qualified to land there.

I've run 15 marathons, but over the years, the wear and tear on my knees eventually forced a switch from running to walking. Now, I hike. Whether it's through the streets of Manhattan or the mountainous terrain of Colorado, the seaside preserves of the Hamptons or 17,000 feet above sea level in Nepal.

There's not much real estate to invest in on the side of Mount Everest. But that's not why you go. Some say you climb it for one simple reason: because it's there. You can make it a bit more personal, of course, setting it as a challenge to beat, a goal to reach, a test to see what you're made of. There's also the notion that, in order to appreciate the world all around you every day, to see it from a new and inspiring perspective, it helps to pack your bags and immerse yourself in a place unlike the one you call home.

When you start this hike on the other side of the world, in the beginning, you're hiking on cobblestones, because the whole transportation mode in Nepal is over these roads that have been traveled for hundreds of years. One of the first things you realize is there are no motor vehicles. Everything moves either on the top of a yak or a porter—the porters carry everything. These porters are the strongest people you've ever met in your life. Going over crevices, they'll grab you by the wrist, and you know that if you fall, they're right there to catch you.

Roads smoothed by countless steps through history and

visions of treacherous deep ravines remain fresh in my mind. So do memories of having breakfast overlooking Everest, of meeting locals and the other people on my tour and sharing stories of their pasts and what brought them to that shared present on the mountain. Of embracing the local culture, the dancing and singing at night, the spectacular warmth of the Himalayan people. And obstacles quite unlike any I had ever encountered.

Early in the hike, I wasn't used to going over swinging bridges. The widest they are is two people wide. You look down hundreds of feet below, and, well, I had to readjust my thinking. I decided I would look straight ahead. I'd never look down.

Cue the dramatic movie music.

You know these bridges, even if you've never ventured across one. Slats of wood, some cracked, some missing, creaking beneath your boots. The only supports are ropes, who knows how old, anchored into the sides of a hill across some drop that falls away into a watery pit or a rocky melee hundreds or thousands of feet below. They sway in the wind, rock side to side under the weight of the people and animals who have no other way to get from place to place.

I remember being on the first bridge—you walk across not as a group, but one at a time—and all of a sudden I see a yak walking toward me from the opposite direction. I'm midway on the bridge and I can't figure out how we're both going to cross. I couldn't go back, the yak is coming at me, there's somebody with a stick behind the yak. So I went to the side, which is all rope, and the yak made it by, and I said if I made it through that, I can make it through anything on this trip.

The swinging bridges aren't as gaudy as their suspension bridge counterparts back home in New York City, but in the Himalayas they've stood the test of time. They are designed for the long term. You won't walk across them quickly, and certainly not without considering the pace of your passage. But when something like a rogue yak comes at you out of nowhere, their design and your approach to crossing will help you manage most tough situations.

Sometimes what's happening is challenging. Sometimes it's overwhelming, because life can be overwhelming. The important lesson is to have a positive attitude, be optimistic that things are going to work out.

Remember that house in Brooklyn way back when—we put 10% down, we went under contract, and we had 30 days to get a mortgage. And for 30 days, I didn't sleep, my wife didn't sleep. It was, *Woe is me, how are we going to do this, we'll owe all this money, oh my god, over $100,000—how are we going to pay it?* I was just starting out in law, and yet somehow I came to believe that I could do it—*I can, I will, I must. I can* *do it, I can do it*—and I did it. That's how I did it.

That's how anyone can do it, climb any mountain, meet any challenge. Attitude and effort.

It's all hard work. If you want to be successful in this life, you have to work at it. You have to *want* to be successful in order to *be* successful. That's the first thing. It doesn't come naturally because you're a genius, it doesn't come naturally because you invented a hundred products. It comes because you worked hard at it. It's experience and hard work.

And then you need luck. It's a small percentage of luck. But the harder you work, the luckier you get.

And the fewer yaks you'll find in your path.

CHAPTER 24

LIVE LIKE YOU WORK, WORK LIKE YOU LIVE

When I was 12 years old, I had my first job. I would get up at 3:30 or 4 in the morning on the weekends, and my brother, who was 17 years older than me, would pick me up. First we would go to the diner, where all the milkmen were, and the people who worked late. It was a wondrous experience for me. Here I am, 12 years old, and I'm in this diner with all these men who are working. I still remember the smells and the talk among them.

The clinks of plates and silverware provided a background rhythm to the chorus of voices wafting through the air, intermingled with thick scents of smoky bacon and bitter coffee, frying eggs and cakes on a greased griddle. Then we'd go to the milk farms and pick up the milk, and deliver it to people's homes.

Galvanized steel milk boxes waited in the dark outside the doors of these homes like night deposit vaults. People would leave a note in the box, whether they wanted cream or this or that. And everything was glass. My brother could handle three bottles in each hand, but because my fingers were small, I could only handle two.

As time went by, not even the world of milk delivery was

insulated from the rush of convenience and products on demand. For a brief blip in dairy history, as packaging transitioned from glass to cardboard, there were milk machines, like the soda machines we use today. My brother had a number of machines on a route, on public corners and at gas stations, where people could drop in 30 or 40 cents and get a carton of milk.

I'll never forget, one day I got a call from my friend and he said, "That milk machine you had downstairs, it's giving free milk!" As soon as one carton would be taken out, another would come down! There was a line of people when I got down there, and I was trying to shoo them away, and they were saying, "Wait your turn, kid, wait your turn!"

I went up to the front of the line and salvaged the remaining cartons of milk, put them in my bike's basket and rode home. In life, the goal isn't just to grab as much milk as you can, of course.

The pursuit of happiness is the basis for everything we do. Many people think that if you have money, you'll be happy, and all your problems will simply go away. But it will only take away your financial problems. You're only going to go through this life once—at least that I'm aware of. So whatever you do, the first thing you have to ask is: What am I trying to achieve? How am I going to achieve it? What will I do to make myself happy?

This is not a situation where you're given three wishes from a genie. You're taking on some serious introspection. You have to seriously consider what would bring you happiness before you go off in its pursuit. Setting goals for yourself is the only way you're going to reach them.

If your goal is to make as much money as you can, well, that's one goal, but I don't think that's going to make you happy. It may, but I don't think so. My advice is to do something that you find interesting. Something that will provide for your family, that will build self-respect and the respect of your peers, something that might offer you an opportunity to give back to charity. And whatever that pursuit might be, it should be complemented by a loving family that's core to your life. Then I think you're well on your way.

I have always found that, in setting personal goals and carving a path toward happiness, it helps to keep other people in mind. As a lawyer, I tried cases for 30 years, day in and day out. I always thought of myself as Robin Hood. I took from the rich insurance companies and I gave to working-class people. They usually used the money for life-changing events, and I loved it. To me, it was almost a religion. The judgments I got for my clients allowed families to send their children to college, to buy their first home. In more cases than you could imagine, it was the first time these people would have money in the bank as opposed to debts and bleak financial futures. Many times I would set up trusts or annuities for them, so they'd have an income for the rest of their lives.

Yes, over time I made money for myself, and my firm. That was an important measure of success. But it never dominated my decision making—not in law, not in real estate, not anywhere.

After about 25 years as a practicing attorney, I became a much more involved alumnus of New York Law School. It was an opportunity to give back in a very personal way. Memories of my mother standing up to my father and giving me the best life she could remain with me to this day. They have ingrained in me the belief that if she could battle and survive, then nothing was impossible for me. I wanted to pay some of that hope and possibility forward, and the first thing I wanted to do was honor my mother and give scholarships to single moms who wanted to go to law school, because I know how insurmountable the odds are. I lived it, I saw it every day—how impossible it is for a single woman to raise children lovingly and caringly and earn a living to support them. It's impossible. Not hard, *impossible*.

Every year the Ruth Schnurman Memorial Scholarship is awarded to a woman undertaking the arduous task of studying law and raising a family on her own. I'll admit that the scholarship does serve something of a selfish end. I do it for myself, because it makes me feel so good. Every year I meet the recipient, and it's also tremendously gratifying to read the letters I receive from prior honorees who've graduated and gone on to fulfill their dreams.

There are people out there—you may even be one of them—who have used the show-stopping speech by actor Michael Douglas in the film *Wall Street* as a motivational tool. Even if you've never seen the movie, there's a good chance you've seen its most famous three words adorning T-shirts and coffee mugs and corporate conference rooms, and not only down where the bulls and bears run. You've heard politicians and hedge fund managers pull it out during speeches and interviews.

"Greed is good."

It's a great line (even if it's actually "Greed, for lack of a better word, is good") in a great scene, no argument there. One of Hollywood's best. It defined the 1980s and it won the guy an Academy Award. More people probably quote that line than anything Shakespeare ever put on paper. It's memorable. But it's not your mantra.

You don't have to be greedy. You don't have to be a bad person. In my opinion, it's the exact opposite. If you want people to trust you, you have to do the right thing by them. You have to be trustworthy, be honorable.

This means looking beyond yourself and assessing the larger impact of your actions. Take the Hamptons as an example, where open plots of dirt seem to rise in scarcity by the hour. Grabbing it all for yourself is not a plan that's going to work. You can do very well for yourself and help others at the same time. Doing good is good.

For every development I did in the Hamptons, I had to set aside two-thirds of the property, to keep it forever as an agricultural reserve for future generations. Two-thirds. Not a quarter. Not just half. Two-thirds. Yes, that's the stipulation I had to abide by in order to get the local government's sign-off that would allow me to build. Another developer might have shouted and sued and tried every which way to get around having to give even an inch of land. *I just paid for 18 acres,* they'll scream, *and you want me to let 12 of them just sit there? They're mine! I'm going to fight this!* And they do.

I like the idea that the land I preserved under the zoning rules will be enjoyed by future generations. They're not making any more land, and if you abuse the land, you're not going to have the land. It's as simple as that. Why shouldn't I help the future? Don't I have an obligation to do that? Don't we all?

Giving back doesn't only mean donating to charity or volunteering your time at a nonprofit. You can make a very wise real estate investment for yourself that also serves the needs of the community. And every community, regardless of wealth both real and perceived, has areas where it can use a helping hand.

Jerry Seinfeld and Steven Spielberg live in East Hampton. So do Beyoncé and Jay-Z, Martha Stewart and more famous faces. Beyond the bold-faced names is a roster of wealthy homeowners you've never heard of but for whom eight-figure summer homes are a drop in the beach bucket. Yet the tony area is not exclusively the domain of millionaires and billionaires and disposable income that seems to challenge the GDP of some nations.

There's a working class in East Hampton, too, providing the services and resources that make the area such a desirable place to live and invest for those in the higher-income brackets. No matter how hard they work, it's not easy for them to live in the community. My partners and I purchased the largest building in the Village of East Hampton because we realized there was a scarcity of apartments for couples and single people working in this mecca of asset-based investors. Whether it's the schoolteachers, the people working in the shops, or people working at healthcare and medical facilities, all these people need a place to live.

Yes, the apartments have consistently generated income, but they've also given people a place they call home. It always comes back to happiness, its pursuit and attainment.

You have to work at it. I actually work at it, at making myself happy. And you have to make not only your mind but your body happy. I exercise every day. I don't run anymore, but I walk significant distances. For me to go out for a walk, it's three hours. I'll go 10 or 12 miles, in all types of weather. I try to eat right. I don't do drugs, I don't smoke, I don't drink—I know it sounds boring to most people. But by taking care of your body, by taking care of your mind, by doing no harm, you gain self-respect. If you want to be happy, you have to have self-respect.

Searching for a deeper understanding of what ties us all together is as thrilling as any other pursuit. Acquiring knowledge is a wonderful thing, but even the quest itself has its rewards. Destinations themselves rarely offer the sense of fulfillment that the journeys provide, especially for those who agree that the unexamined life is something of a waste.

I try to learn. I read inspirational books, spiritual books, motivational books. I'm always trying to find the answer— whether it's a Zen or Buddhist direction or something else—to what we're all about. Science tells us the elements that we're made of return to the cosmos, and I have faith, although maybe not the same as others. I believe there's something going on that I don't have the capacity to understand, but I do believe it's something. It may not be a person who looks like us, it may not be something we call god. But I do believe there's a superior force—not being, force—holding the entire universe together.

I'm always searching for those answers that I don't know— to what this life is about, why we're here. The answers must coincide with our goals. To lead a good life. A happy life. An enriched life. *The goal is to respect yourself.*

That self-respect will, in turn, reflect outward onto others. Even when you're on opposite sides of the table.

CHAPTER 25

TWO SIDES OF ONE TABLE

The woman and her boy step to the edge of the sidewalk as the city bus pulls up to the stop at this Brooklyn street corner. The doors open with their attendant hiss and the driver casts a disinterested look as the pair steps on board. He sees mothers and sons getting on an off all day, every day.

Just not mothers like this one.

The woman and her son are traveling only a few blocks, she tells the driver as he pulls back into the flow of traffic. Surely they should not really have to pay the fare, or at least not all of it. *Look, lady,* he replies, *it makes no difference if you go two or three blocks or you go to the end of the line, it's the same price.* She continues the discussion, her accent not Russian but Ukrainian, and the bus rolls on.

Perhaps not the full fare, she suggests, but a portion, maybe. The driver, pulling to the next stop, continues to insist that the full fare is all he can accept. He is midsentence as he opens the doors to accept his next passengers, and the mother, having arrived where she wanted to get off, takes the staring boy by the hand as they disembark.

Even more than 60 years later, that memory makes me laugh. That bus driver never had a chance. My mother was the best negotiator I've ever met in my life, up to this very day. She would negotiate anything.

Bus fares, mattresses, clothing, you name it. Store owners would chase her out into the street to complete a sale, bewildered as to what had just transpired during a negotiation for some particular item. The skill my mother possessed was an acquired one, invented as a means of survival for a woman who came to the United States from a small town outside Kiev when she was only 12. She had to fend for herself with three children, and every dime was so important.

Had Ruth Schnurman been born into society now, not only would she have realized her dream of being a clothing designer, she would surely have been one of note. She knew what she wanted and needed, and understood that there was a way to talk to people, to persuade and reason, amid the give and take it would require to get things done within her means and to her satisfaction. I admired many aspects of my mother's personality, and her skill in communication was among those I admired most.

Yes, communication is a skill like any other. Some people are naturally better at it than others, but everyone can learn how to master it. In almost any profession, this will serve you well. To invest in real estate, you'll need to speak with individuals—homeowners, brokers, attorneys, tenants—as well as to groups. You may be meeting a team of investors or bankers you're asking to finance your deal, or a town board you need to convince to let you develop a property under their jurisdiction. You can learn and polish this skill in whatever career you have now, then apply it elsewhere.

Being a litigating attorney taught me to speak in front of groups. Being a lawyer is trying to explain your client's claim to the jury. It taught me how to speak publicly and to argue my client's case. It also taught me how to negotiate, because basically that's what I did—I negotiated multiple cases every single day. Ninety percent of the cases were settled before a verdict, so it was a matter of negotiating.

Negotiating isn't synonymous with dominating, mind you. Yes, your interests are at the fore, but in most cases, you don't need to be playing a zero-sum game. J. Paul Getty isn't necessarily among my notable quotables, but the guy made a good point when he said, "You must never try to make all the money that's in a deal. Let the other fellow make some money too, because if you have a reputation for always making all the money, you won't have many deals."

Your reputation is all you have at the end of the day. It characterizes the way you've dealt with people and projects in the past, which in turn gives both longtime partners and brand new prospects alike a clear picture of what they can expect from you. For those who don't know you or your work yet, or if you're just starting out and haven't built a reputation that precedes you, your demeanor at the negotiating table, and every table leading up to that one, should be one of respect and confidence. Know what you want, know what the other side wants, and know that how you arrive at the final agreement—which could wind up being an agreement to not do business together—is not going to be forgotten, for better or for worse.

The key element of negotiating is that there has to be credibility and trust between all parties. It's very, very difficult without that feeling of mutual trust. Very rarely will you come to a resolution. That's why most business people, when they first meet—let's assume it's dinner— they don't start negotiating until dessert. Because you spend all of dinner learning about each other—where you live, where you work, your family, your children, your vacation or whatever—and then you negotiate. You have to establish a rapport.

You're a human being, and the person on the other side is a human being. They may be a celebrity, they may be 10 times wealthier than you, it makes no difference— everybody is the same. Everybody has insecurity, everybody feels that they wish they could do better in certain fields, and if you trust yourself, you'll do very well. The key element in negotiation—just like it's location, location, location in real estate—is credibility and trustworthiness.

There are many ways to build that credibility and trust. But if you think you're going to win a negotiation by intimidation, you're sadly mistaken. No banker wants to be intimidated, no buyer wants to be intimidated, no seller wants to be intimidated. You can't intimidate anyone in this life and then go back again and again. You just can't do it.

There is, of course, a distinct difference between intimidation and standing your ground. Your research and due diligence have told you exactly what you need in order to make your project work for you. That may be price, it may be timing, it may be location. You may want to own a certain property in the worst way. You may be convincing yourself that nothing like it will ever come along again, and maybe you'll sacrifice something to close the deal. That's your decision, but be very careful before you run down that road.

I've walked away from real estate deals when negotiations were going in the wrong direction. One of my tenets of real estate is to never chase a deal. There's always another deal. You want to be able to walk away.

Remember, this is real estate, it's not love. It's a business. We don't get attached to real estate. We get attached to each other.

CHAPTER 26

SO YOU WANT TO BE A LANDLORD

"It's always better to be a landlord than a tenant."

—*Alan Schnurman*

"This is the business we've chosen."

—*Hyman Roth*

Walking down Fulton Street in the late 1980s, you would typically see families strolling the sidewalks, shops opening for business, people coming and going up and down the subway steps on journeys to Manhattan or deeper into Brooklyn. Above one particular subway stop rose a building, five stories of apartments, and if you looked closely, you might notice a slight bulge in the wall facing Fulton. Nothing that would really concern anyone, just a physical anomaly.

I lived in Park Slope, not terribly far from this building I'd purchased in the 1980s. Being geographically close to my investments has always been important, particularly in the early years. The building was filled with renters, and I would go by it often, sometimes with my children in tow. Rents were good, the tenants were good, the value of the property was going up. All was right and quiet and steady in this unassuming corner of the world.

Then the phone rang.

I got a call saying, "Alan, the fire department is here! You have to come down right away!"

I came down, and there was the entire wall of the building, all the bricks, lying scattered in the street. I stood there among the crowd and the rubble, looking up in disbelief at where the façade had been mere hours before, staring into the building's innards like it was some kind of life-size urban dollhouse.

You could look into everybody's apartment. They had painted them all different colors, you could see their bedrooms—it was surreal. Someone had called the fire department, they'd evacuated the whole building. The whole street was closed. It was just terrible. Thank god no one was hurt.

I remember somebody came over and said, "Is this your building?" And I said "No, I only work for the guy."

Humor aside, this is one of those moments that will make you wonder, is it worth it being a landlord? It's impossible to foresee every challenge of owning a building, and you have to be able to face the issues as they arise. When the unpredictable happens, attitude and optimism—and smart financial planning—will help you through. *I can, I will, I must.*

We rebuilt that façade. But a year later, when a fire struck the first floor of the same building, that was it. Call it a curse, an omen, call it whatever you want, but my partners and I decided to sell—and that remains the only piece of Brooklyn real estate, aside from my first home, that I ever let go.

TIME WORKS FOR YOU

Despite your best efforts, the properties you rent out aren't all going to be winners, as falling walls and fires prove. Others will pay off, but perhaps not right away. You already know that success is not an overnight thing. In some situations, it may take years. In the case of one particular building in downtown Manhattan—and at five stories and 10,000 square feet, no small undertaking—it took me a quarter-century.

This one started off as a terrible project almost before the ink was dry. Not exactly in a walls-came-tumbling-down kind of way, but for years my partner Ben and I had to feed the project. There wasn't enough income to pay the expenses. We used to only rent that building to musicians and creative people, because lofts were not in favor. But I don't give up on anything.

This particular area of Manhattan was, at the time I bought it, not what you'd call "chic." The expensive restaurants and bars that now line the streets were nonexistent. High-priced hotels were not even something people dreamt about. It was desirable to the artist community because the price was right. But I saw potential.

All then in the blink of an eye, it became very fashionable. People wanted lofts, they wanted space, they wanted the light. At the time the rents weren't anything to write home about, but 25 years later, I could live off the income.

I want to be able to carry my properties without any rent for at least two years. I'm a very conservative investor, so I never overly leverage. If we're in the worst recession, I want to be a buyer, not a seller. If you look at very successful people, they always keep a lot of cash in the bank. It's part of their success. Remember, I don't buy to flip, I buy to hold, I buy to improve. As I've mentioned, I have sold a number of properties shortly after I purchased them, but only because I've gotten offers I couldn't refuse.

YOU'RE GOING TO CHARGE WHAT?

Figuring out what you're going to charge for rent follows the same process as figuring out what market you're going to invest in and what properties within that market are best for you. When the time comes, you'll be able to figure it out.

How, you ask? You've done your due diligence. You've looked on the internet and even in the local papers, you've gone around with brokers and inquired about rental comps. So you now know basically what people are asking, and thus what you'll be asking.

There's a chance you've heard rules and equations for determining what a rent should be. You'd do well to toss them out the nearest window. One size does not fit all.

There's no magic formula, no single approach, because every neighborhood is different. *Real estate is all local.* That means that Garden City on Long Island may be a hot area, and Massapequa may be stagnant, although they're only 20 miles apart. Fifteen years ago, Manhattan's Lower East Side needed improvement. Now, the area is white hot. Chelsea, Harlem and Washington Heights may be on fire, but you might cross the river to New Jersey and find the market is flat.

Regardless of where you're a landlord, there's one constant. Change. Even in a luxury marketplace, where trends may have endured for decades, that change will rear its head. Property owners in the Hamptons, for example, used to be able to rely on a rental market filling up from Memorial Day to Labor Day as if the trend were part of some natural cycle. It's a summer-centric community, and renters followed the calendar like migrating birds or fish—year in, year out.

Then, as 2010 edged toward 2020, the plates began to shift.

The advent of options like AirBNB, for example, changed the way many people travel, inspiring them to rent for shorter periods of time, weekends or weeks, and to explore different locations rather than setting down roots in any one spot. At the high end of the Hamptons market, people are still willing to spend more than $250,000 for the July through August season. I know, I know. It's hard to believe, but in the Hamptons you're talking about the richest people in the United States, and you'd be amazed how many there are. And they all want to be in the same place. Finding those high-end renters just takes a little more work than it did in the past.

That's why I've diversified within the market. In the Hamptons, the apartments and small houses bring rent year-round. In East Hampton, in the building from the chapter "Love, Love Me Due Diligence," we have eight one-bedroom apartments, three retail stores, plus four garages. We also have a four-bedroom house next door that we gut renovated and now rent out—even when there's snow on the ground.

RESIDENTIAL VS. RETAIL

You don't have to choose. I've done well in both residential and retail, and there's always opportunity down either path. Over time, having both in your portfolio can prove to be a valuable way to diversify.

In retail, I have a fondness for service businesses. They're consistent, reliable and provide a service to the community that gives them an element of staying power. One of my most successful storefronts, in fact, is a pediatrician in Brooklyn. Yes, doctors are a service industry. They'll always need a physical space from which to work. This is how you need to be thinking when looking into retail space as a prospective landlord.

The internet has already changed retail as we know it. But services—restaurants, workout places like CrossFit, a bakery, a nail salon—those are doing fairly well, as opposed to retail such as clothing, which can be bought online.

COLLECTING YOUR MONEY

You become a landlord because, from a business perspective, you can make money by renting out a property. Or at least it will allow you to draw some income while the value of the property itself increases over time. In either case, you'll be making an ongoing investment of time and money, whether it's doing maintenance, making improvements, dealing with legal issues, or surrounding yourself with a solid support team.

So, if the tenant can't or won't give you that money, there's something of a problem afoot. Surely you've heard stories about people who don't pay their rent. Retail or residential, long term or short term, you have to set up a process that will keep the cash flowing in and which gives you some modicum of protection.

We'll start with a relatively easy one.

You have a property you want to rent out to would-be vacationers. It will be a few weeks, maybe a month or a summer (or, if you're in ski country, winter) season.

My number one rule: On a vacation home, you get the money up front, so you don't have to worry about the financial stability.

The concept is fairly simple to embrace. Before you hand over the keys or the keypad code, the cash is in hand, the check has cleared or the credit card has been approved. Your money is in the bank, and the renters are set for a fabulous holiday.

Now, if it's going to be longer than a few weeks or months, and the payments are going to be spread out over time rather than paid in an up-front lump sum, you're going to want more security than simply somebody's word and a handshake. Those are great, and most people—we have to hope—are good to their word. You need more than that, however.

When you're renting on a long-term basis and you're getting paid monthly, you do a credit check. And you don't rent to a person who has a bad credit rating—but it doesn't begin and end there. As you may have guessed, there are a number of reasons you won't be saying yes to everyone who might want to rent your space.

SCREEN TEST

Your desire is to establish a positive landlord-tenant relationship, ideally one that will last for years. I've rented one of my Bridgehampton homes to the same family for more than 13 years now. You don't need to become best friends, but you want mutual respect, smooth and cordial interactions and transactions. One of the great things about being a landlord is the range of people you'll get to meet, the myriad businesses and tenants you'll be able to provide a place to work and live and find success and happiness. As this is a two-way street, your success and happiness are not less important than that of the tenant.

When screening prospective tenants, you'll do background checks, get eviction reports and credit reports. You're entitled to contact a tenant's employer and other sources as references. You'll interview them, and preferably face-to-face (a real estate broker you know and trust can help in this screening effort). You must also be aware that there are a number of questions you cannot legally ask prospective tenants. Issues of discrimination and fair housing are vitally important, and are changing all the time. These are best left for you to discuss with your attorney than to be detailed in this book.

As a landlord, I have one cardinal rule: *Get references from former landlords, and take their feedback very seriously.* This applies anywhere, any time, regardless of your market or the money on the table.

In the Hamptons and Aspen, my tenants are among the richest people in the United States. They pay good money, and they pay on time. But money isn't the only factor. You know that you can't buy happiness. In some cases, you can't even rent it out.

I won't rent to a person who's had a bad landlord experience, because normally things don't change. *(This would be the exception to my rule about the only constant being change, of course.)* When I did make an exception, it wound up being one of the worst experiences I've ever had.

In this instance, I'd had a warning from a prior landlord, but I said, "No, I can handle it. They're paying top dollar, I've done this for so long and dealt with all kinds of people." But there simply was no satisfying them.

Every day there was a different issue. I would solve one problem, and they would go on to the next one. It was a daily occurrence. It got to a point where I was ready to evict them. I'm an excellent landlord, and I try to satisfy every need. If something needs replacing, I try to handle it right away. They would treat contractors who came to the house with disdain. There was no placating this tenant.

Ultimately I had to have someone else take it over. This kind of thing happens with a very small percentage of people, but it does happen.

WHERE DID ALL MY HANGERS GO?

When you're a landlord, the calls are going to come. Ideally, the person on the other end will be making reasonable requests. And they won't be shouting that walls are coming down. But be prepared for matters to arise that need to be addressed. The AC is out, the heat won't come on, the toilet isn't flushing, the lawn isn't mowed. A pack of dead squirrels is stuffing up the chimney.

Depending on the arrangement, these can all be the landlord's burden to carry. For this reason, it's important to set your rules and parameters at the outset. This goes for what you expect as well as what your tenant expects. If you don't want smoking or pets, then say so. This will help with the screening process, and it will prevent unpleasant situations from arising down the road.

It's also one of the reasons I use a broker when renting my properties, as opposed to going the AIRBNB route. AIRBNB is very lucrative, but a broker creates a buffer between you and the renter. I like that, because most of my renters are on the high end. It makes you unseen, and a broker can help fix issues that arise.

Make no mistake, though. You'll be handling the ultimate fixes yourself, because it's your property, your business.

I consider myself a brick-and-mortar guy. That means when the toilet is broken, or there's a problem with the roof, I get somebody to fix it. Every single day I have problems—but I don't call them problems, I call them "challenges." If you're not ready to accept that real estate is a business and there are issues every single day, then it's not for you. Things will inevitably go wrong. In the long run, of course, it's worth it.

Let's say, for instance, that a sewage backup is threatening to push unspeakable foulness through floors and walls and any accessible crack or crevice at your property. In particularly rough moments like this, I seek solace in a quote. This one, however, isn't from a renowned financier, or even Helen Keller. Try Hyman Roth.

You might know it, actually. Roth, the Meyer Lansky–inspired mobster in *The Godfather Part II*, is discussing how his associate Moe Greene had been killed, part of the spiraling mob violence. "I let it go," Roth says. "Because this is the business we've chosen."

Sitting there in that house, waiting for the aforementioned sewage issue to be resolved, I took a picture and sent it to my kids, with the caption, "This is the business we've chosen."

In some cases, the property will present the challenges. In others, it will be the tenants themselves. I'd say 95% of all tenants and renters are fine. But you have to be prepared for anything. There will even be situations where things go missing. Most of the time there will be a reasonable explanation. In some cases, renters will have somebody else come and pack everything up for them, and they accidentally take all your towels, or some such thing. Once, I probably had 150 hangers in a house, and someone took them all. Why on earth would you take all the hangers?

Part of your job is also finding a balance between maintaining the quality of your property and ensuring its future rentability. How much work will it take to rent it to the next person once the current tenant leaves? You want to give tenants a feeling of personal pride that comes from the property being "theirs," at least in a sense. On a long-term rental, how much will you allow them to personalize the home, such as hanging artwork or the like? Can they dig up part of the yard to plant a vegetable garden?

Now be prepared. Some renters will have more of a sense of entitlement than others. It's not unheard of for short-term renters in vacation areas like the Hamptons to ask for soap, towels, garbage pickup and other services you'd never imagine. If they're not part of the deal, say so. After all, you didn't get into this business to be running a hotel.

Or did you?

CHAPTER 27

CHECK-IN TIME

Let's pause here a moment to recalibrate the image of the Hamptons that you may have in your head, if you've never visited. There's no scarcity of over-the-top mansions, as you've read and have by now likely perused online. There's no dearth of personal fortune. If you check out those *Forbes* rankings, do a little experiment and crosscheck it against the number of those elite who own homes in the Hamptons. There's no shortage of fine restaurants or top-shelf shops or world-class automobile collections or international equestrian champions or...

Before we work ourselves into a fever pitch, let me tell you one thing the Hamptons is *not* known for. Surprisingly, the area is *not* home to a gaggle, or even a handful, of over-the-top resorts. Small hotels and motels, the occasional inn or bed-and-breakfast—these dot the landscape along both back roads and main highways.

The tallest building of any kind is a mere six stories, and there's only one of those, built by legendary developer Carl Fisher in the 1930s out in Montauk, a town affectionately called The End for its geographic isolation at the tip of Long Island. A fascinating entrepreneur who, among other exploits, opened what may be the first auto dealership in America, Fisher was one of the principal real estate investors, developers and promoters of Miami Beach, where high-rises now dominate the waterfront landscape. He had visions of making Montauk the Miami Beach of the north, but the stock market crash of 1929 put an end to those dreams, and likely kept the skyscraper culture from infiltrating Long Island's East End.

In late 2015, one of the brokers in my real estate office told me about a potential deal. A hotel was for sale, the owners were asking $4.5 million but the numbers were down, and to say it was a shambles would be generous.

You may remember from earlier in this tale that the hotel rests atop a small rise on the south side of the highway just as you enter the Hamptons from the west. For many decades there had been a famous restaurant, the decidedly low-key Lobster Inn fish house, just across the street, an unassuming waterside seafood spot known for a dish called Splat. Four Seasons or Ritz Carlton country this was not. What it was, though, was an opportunity. I always wanted to own a hotel, so I said I'd take a look. And, sure enough, it was as advertised—in disrepair, but the numbers were good. I talked with one of my partners, and we decided to buy it.

If you've never read Herman Wouk's *Don't Stop the Carnival,* you should get yourself a copy and crack it open the minute you finish reading this. There's laughter and tears and a cautionary tale in the travails of Norman Paperman, a New

York City press agent who ditches his big city existence and buys a hotel on the fictional Caribbean island of Amerigo, determined that being a hotelier is his ticket to paradise. If I haven't taught you the importance of doing your due diligence, Mr. Paperman surely will.

I'd never owned a hotel before. I had no experience whatsoever. So I worked the numbers continuously, going over and over and over them. Remember, when I do a new deal, I never look to see how much I'm going to make. I always say, What is my risk, how much can I lose on this deal? And every way I looked at it, I couldn't lose money. I knew if I stayed on top of it, if I stayed on top of the market, I would do very well. And I did.

The key to running a hotel is to be hands-on and pay close attention to the market. It's like any real estate situation—if you're going to fight a market, you have to have very deep pockets and a long-term horizon. I do have a long-term horizon, but I also price my products accordingly.

All in all, I'm happy with the margins. You price a hotel according to the quality of the rooms and the location. This location is very good. It's near the highway but it's a little farther out. It can take you a few minutes to get to town, so you take less money—and people understand that. So my guests are doing well, because they're getting nice, neat rooms at a reasonable rate, and I'm doing well because I essentially remain fully rented.

Price and well-kept rooms are only part of the equation. Any hotel guest, regardless of the price you're paying or the part of the world you're visiting, will say that service and overall experience are as important as any other factor.

My partners and I like the hotel business. We purchased our second hotel in upstate New York, outside Saratoga Springs. When I met the team of 10 staff at the hotel, I told them, *I* can't make this a successful enterprise—it's *you*. I can give you a wonderful building, I can give you fabulous interiors, but you're on the firing line every day. If you don't provide guests with the service that you yourself would want at a hotel, they'll never come back. You'd never come back.

When I speak with that team, or anyone I employ, I never use the phrase "work for me." I always say "work *with* me."

One small word. One big difference.

No matter what project you're talking about, and this could be at the beginning or many years in, you may be the driving force, but understand that you are not the only force. It's a team effort. Everyone works for the enterprise, because if the enterprise is successful, then you will be successful.

"Team" is a notion that too few managers, bosses, name your I'm-in-charge title, understand, or— more to the point—care to understand. Even if you're the owner, standing there at the very top, you're part of a team. And if you're going to lead the individuals to greater heights— which is a core ingredient of a successful venture— remember my three favorite letters.

R.A.P.

Recognition. Appreciation. Praise.

It's a philosophy that applies to any business, large or small, fledgling or established, and it boils down to how you communicate with every staff member. Their daily tasks and responsibilities will vary, but every one of them will thrive. *Recognition, appreciation and praise.* Do it publically, so their peers and coworkers witness the R.A.P., and do it privately as well.

Now, you may be thinking to yourself that there are letters missing from the formula. There's no *M* for money. No *D* for dollars. No *B* for bonus. That's exactly right. Fair and just compensation is important, but it's only part of the bigger picture. I don't care what salary you're paying people, or how wealthy you make them. If you don't express appreciation, recognition and praise, you're missing a variable in the equation.

There's a school that says you need to hold the whip. But let me tell you something: It didn't work in Egypt, and it doesn't work today.

When I bought the hotel in Southampton, I kept the two managers who were already onboard, and when I bought a hotel in Saratoga Springs, about three hours north of New York City, I hired a management team. But I still remain involved. I like that touchy-feely thing. If I buy something, I like to be able to drive to it, to look at it.

Historically, the best real estate areas are New York City, Aspen, the Hamptons, and I'm involved in all three. I also have projects in Brooklyn, and one in New Jersey. Saratoga and upstate New York is a new frontier, but probably not the last.

Denver is another market I'd consider, both residential and long-term commercial. They built Denver International Airport, one of the largest airports in the west, which can accommodate an incredible amount of traffic. It's become a major hub, easy in and easy out. A lot of young people are moving into the Denver-Boulder area since it's a burgeoning tech center. That's a critical component to the economy, so wherever you see that type of job growth, and young people moving in, it's an area you want to consider, because there is a long-term growth effect.

I never believed in Florida as an investment target, largely because of the boom-or-bust nature of the market. Now the boom-bust nature of nature itself makes the area even more tenuous. The impact of climate change is something I am studying very closely. I applaud places as far apart geographically and psychologically as Seattle, with its reputation of addressing environment issues, and New York City, which has begun to take a leadership role among cities facing the threat of rising seas.

I believe in global warming, I believe in climate change, so I usually try to follow my belief systems and stay ahead of the curve. I don't believe that it's really going to affect me in my lifetime significantly, other than storms, but I believe it will affect my grandchildren greatly. I believe it may be one of the major issues in the future for our species.

As for those who refuse to embrace the science staring them in the face, who deny the potential coming climatological catastrophes that seem undeniable, I don't quite understand their position. Maybe they know something I don't?

CHAPTER 28

A MAN AND HIS GOATS

This is a very, very special place. I cannot help but think that, feel that, every time I'm here.

I've made a great deal of real estate purchases in my career. There's one, however, that gives me perhaps more pleasure than any other—an environment where even I am continually amazed. A friend once called it the best purchase decision I've ever made.

The Farm.

Now, you've heard me advise against falling in love with real estate. And that adage holds true. But, to turn to the quote jar one more time, I'll tip my hat to women's rights advocate Margaret Fuller, who said, "Nature provides exceptions to every rule."

Up to this point, farms and off-the-beaten-path locales haven't been much a part of our discussion. There have been opulent mansions, billionaire ski slope getaways, apartments and multi-use buildings in the most dynamic city in the world…but never has a farm come up.

And why would it? What would a city kid from Brooklyn know, or want to know, about farming?

Quite a great deal, as fate would have it.

As 2010 moved toward mid-decade and 2015 inched ever closer to 2020, hindsight and foresight converged around a very particular point. The past and the future are always intertwined in my mind, one informing the other, whether on a real estate deal or other business venture or any aspect of life. I decided to diversify again, in upstate New York. Where, of course, was the question.

I wanted to keep it within a two-hour radius of New York City, because I figured any farther than that and my children and grandchildren wouldn't make use of it. So I drew a circle around New York and I started looking for a farm that I could make self-sustaining through alternate energy means—solar and perhaps geothermal. I wanted a farm that had fresh water running through it.

I searched for two years, poring over listings and never finding anything that felt, well, special. But persistence pays off. One day, there in my search, it appeared. As I looked through the pictures of a farm on the border of Duchess and Columbia County, all rolling hills and bucolic beauty about two hours outside Manhattan, something in me stirred. I called the listing broker and asked if I could come see it in person.

"Terrific," she said. "I'll put together five or six locations to look at."

"No, I only want to see this farm," I said. I drove up and got there early, and I sat in the driveway. Just sitting there, looking at the farm from the driveway, I knew I was going to buy it.

I bought a mountain! How many people do you know who can say that?

When I first walked the 120-acre property—which quickly increased to nearly 130 acres when I purchased an adjacent lot—it was more magnificent than I'd ever imagined. Of course, I knew nothing about farms or farming. But there wasn't even a moment's hesitation. Over the years, as I searched for a property upstate, I'd continually done—say it with me now—my due diligence. And I did more of it for this farm than for almost any property I've ever purchased.

I researched different types of products you can grow on a farm, depending on the region. I spoke to several farmers. Cornell University has an actual farm division in Duchess County, and I met with the head of that institution, who handles these types of properties, and she gave me her suggestions as to what I could do with the land.

One option was dairy, because I'm adjacent to a very large dairy farm, or meat cattle. But of course, since I'm a vegan, that didn't sit very well.

For now, the farmer who'd worked on the property for 13

years prior remains there to care for the land, keeping the place running until the future comes into focus. Honestly, I'm in no rush to decide.

Patience, patience, patience. The quality of the location is unequivocal, so time is now the other part of the equation. And if any property was meant to be held for the long haul, it's this one. These 130 acres will hopefully provide a retreat and refuge, be a source of joy for my family for as many generations as time will allow. The goal, beyond being an active, productive farm, is to be a real estate investment that will grow in value.

Yes, this is an investment. That shouldn't be forgotten amid all the rhapsodic praise. Keeping the personal and business aspects of any deal separate is a challenge for any investor, myself included. It's easy to get emotional about a property, which is not necessarily a bad thing as long as the business side of your deal remains calculatedly in its place.

Any changes I have in mind for The Farm are in line with creating that family oasis for the future. I have no illusions that whatever changes we'll make will come easily, and I look forward to whatever challenges may arise. It's the challenges, and how you handle them, that determine whether or not you'll have a successful life.

There is, without a doubt, a self-sustainability to The Farm that appeals to me, to a part of me that I've tapped into in order to go places others said I couldn't, or shouldn't. That Thoreau-eque sense of self-reliance is inherent on The Farm, organic in a way that other places and their potential investors could never imagine.

Here, the amenities are…different. There's a horse farm and stable, and about 25 chickens. I have two goats! I have an organic garden, and two acres of orchards, apples and peaches. I have eight stacks of beehives. I have a stream on the property, and four ponds. The adjacent lot I purchased is a wooded property on a hill that was a maple farm at one time. Not that I'm going into the maple syrup business, but it's good to know. I have trails that go through the woods. It's never-ending. It's like Disney World.

The Farm just might be the happiest place on earth. Inside the five miles of fencing that define this magical little kingdom, there are also nine paddocks, three barns, a main house, a guest house, and—perhaps my favorite amenity of all—space. Seemingly endless swaths of space. Even in the surrounding town, it has an impact on the way people live among one another, in the best possible way.

You go to the grocery store and they say hello to you. They don't even have scanners at checkout! It's very personal and very close, almost like an extended-family atmosphere. It's hard to believe that only two hours from one of the world's major urban centers there's this location that's so totally different. And there's all this breathing room. Warm people and wide-open spaces.

Every morning I walk a four-mile loop near the property, a stroll that takes me up on a mountain, passing two dairy farms and a cattle farm. Sometimes I'll even spot the occasional sheep. It's my time to soak in the wonder of the natural beauty all around.

Then I go into the tree house—for the grandchildren, I built a beautiful tree house in a tangle of trees, but I think I like it more than they do—and I meditate for 10 minutes. When the weather is good, I do it on the deck of the tree house. If the weather is a little chilly, I do it inside.

You may wonder how meditating might suit a person like me, who has a hard time sitting still. But in order to keep your mind full of new ideas, I believe you have to empty it regularly.

Think of your brain as a railroad station, and trains are constantly arriving and departing. When you meditate, you focus on just being the station, without any trains going in or out. You'd be surprised if you do it just 10 minutes a day, it gives you such a replenishing feeling. That's what happens when I'm at The Farm.

I cannot fully capture all the emotions and sensations that come with this place. Recharging, restful, reinvigorating, renewing…they aren't wrong, but not quite right.

Rejuvenation doesn't even exactly capture it, but it's close. It's a physical thing and a psychological thing and something beyond all that. Maybe the inability to define it is a definition in itself.

* * *

At 4:30 a.m., the hills of New York's Hudson Valley hold promise in a way few get to see. Fog rising and rolling and shadow figures moving slowly in the distance. Unseen barn doors creaking and maybe the clatter of a gate closing too quickly, dark giving way to day. There is a pulse, The Farm shaking off the cobwebs of sleep, a time when most of the world hasn't had a chance to do very much, or hasn't even tried.

Each day I'm here, I slip out of the farmhouse and become part of these Before Hours, among the rolling grass and trees and mountaintops stretching skyward all around. I'm a solitary figure and very much alone, taking it all in, the natural wonder all around me. Weather, season, they make no difference. I'm out there, every single morning.

I can. I will. I...

Appendix

I CAN, I WILL, I MUST REDUX

I can, I will, I must.

Attitude equals altitude. Always try to have a good attitude no matter what is happening.

Optimism is the faith that leads to achievement. Nothing can be done without hope and confidence.

If I say it, I can believe it.

There is no substitute for experience.

Every single day I have problems—but I don't call them problems, I call them challenges.

If you have no patience, if you don't have a long-term horizon, real estate's not for you. Buy stocks. You'll never be happy in real estate.

A market will turn against you before it turns for you.

I am not interested in today's newspaper article on market conditions. I want to read tomorrow's papers.

It's all hard work. If you want to be successful in this particular life, you have to work at it. You have to want to be successful. That's the first thing. You have to *want* to be successful to *be* successful.

There's risk in everything—if there wasn't, everybody would do it.

I pick my partners very, very, very carefully. You want to always deal with nice people, and you have to be very careful, because a bad partner, like a bad marriage, can be very challenging.

For my happiness, it's family first—it's the center of your universe—and everything else is background.

Finding the best real estate location is just like the circular rings when you throw a pebble in a pond. The best location is where the rock hit the water. The best locations go up first and go down last.

All real estate is local.

It's hard work for a person to realize how good they really are. And who amongst us appreciates how good they really are?

Real estate is creative. I'm not an artist, I'm not a sculptor, I'm not a musical talent. However, with all that said, buying a piece of land, hiring an architect, working with a builder, working with an interior decorator, working with a site planner, working with a surveyor, working with a land expert to figure out the best possible use of that property—

it's all creative process.

When I'm cryin', I should be buyin'.

The key element of negotiating is that there has to be credibility and trust between the parties negotiating.

No one wants to be intimidated by you. Nobody. No one likes to do things because they're intimidated. They'll do it once, but they won't do it twice.

Never chase a deal. There's always another deal. You want to be able to walk away from every single deal. Remember, it's real estate, it's not love. It's real estate. It's a business. We don't get attached to the real estate. We get attached to each other.

You have to listen to the markets. I never fight a market.

In real estate, everybody knows location, location, location. But I always say that after location, location, location comes patience, patience, patience.

My favorite expression for employees is R.A.P.: Recognition, Appreciation, Praise. If you don't express to them the appreciation, the recognition and the praise, well, I think that's all almost as important as compensation.

There's a school that says you need to hold the whip. It didn't work in Egypt, and it doesn't work today.

First, you have to do what I call your due diligence. First, you have to do your homework. First, you have to do the 95% perspiration before you get to the 5% inspiration.

Never buy the improvement, always the land. What goes up in real estate is the value of the land.

It's always a good time to buy real estate…if you have the right location. And the right attitude.

If I knew the right time to buy real estate, we wouldn't be living in New York City right now, we'd be living in Schnurmanville.

I have drawers full of two things: properties that I didn't buy and they've gone up 3 times, or properties that I've sold and they've gone up 10 times. But in real estate, true professionals never look back. I never look back.

When I sell a project that the other person makes a lot of money on, the first thing I say is, good for them!

The 15th marathon is just as hard as the first marathon.

When you set the goal, it's not the achievement of the goal, it's the road to the goal that's so wonderful.

If you're not content to grow rich slowly, you probably won't.

No market moves in one direction. The trend is up on a

long-term basis, but you have to have a long-term view.

It's always better to be a landlord than a tenant.

There's nothing wrong with any of your goals, but you have to understand what your goals are, and you don't want to deviate.

Success and relationships are tied together.

You do create your own luck by being patient.

All advertising works, and you never ever know where a client or a sale comes from.

I'm always searching for the right answer, I'm always searching for those answers that I do not know, on what this life is about, why are we here, and what is the best way to lead a life to be happy. Isn't that our goal? To lead a good life. A happy life. An enriched life. The goal is to respect yourself.

Never be scared of failing, never be scared of making mistakes, because it's part of the process of success. You show me a successful person who's willing to fail and I'll say he's on his way to bigger things.

The fundamentals of real estate investing were true 200 years ago, are true today, and will be true 200 years from today.

I say this in all modesty—I have no original thoughts. If you're looking for someone who's a genius, you have to go somewhere else.

Teamwork makes the dream work.

I can, I will, I must.

About the Author

Alan Schnurman

Alan Schnurman is a real estate investor, attorney and broker in the Hamptons and New York City. He is best know to the public for his distinguished legal background via the 1800Lawline.com firm Zalman Schnurman & Miner, for which he was a founding partner; and the PBS TV legal news program *Lawline*, which he launched in 1983. It continued for 28 years.

He has purchased, developed and sold some of the most significant properties in the Hamptons over the last 30 years. His real estate experience includes: land development, multi-family, hospitality, retail, mixed-use and office properties. In addition to the Hamptons, his investments extend to Manhattan, Brooklyn, Hudson Valley, Saratoga Springs, New Jersey and Aspen.

After four decades as a trial attorney, he retired and joined Saunders & Associates as a real estate broker in the Hamptons. He has received numerous professional honors, including the "Lifetime Achievement Award" presented by the Hon. Jonathan Lippman, Chief Judge of the State of New York on behalf of the NYC Trial Lawyers Association. In 1999, he started Lawline.com, one of the first websites devoted to Continuing Legal Education. It remains the industry leader with over 2,500,000 credits completed.

In addition to hosting his own television program, *Lawline*, he has appeared on the *Today* show, *Good Morning America* and CNN and has been interviewed by *The New York Times*, *The Wall Street Journal* and the *New York Post* for expert comment on real estate and law.

A native of Brooklyn, Alan graduated from New York Law School, where he currently sits on the Board of Trustees and has endowed a scholarship for single mothers in memory of his own mother, Ruth. He has been married to his wife, Judy, for 45 years and they have two children and five grandchildren. Alan is also active physically. He is a vegan, exercises daily, has run 15 marathons and has trekked to the Mount Everest and Patagonia regions, New Zealand and rafted 275 miles through the Grand Canyon (twice).

About the Author

Eric Feil

Eric Feil is the COO and Editorial Director at Dan's Hamptons Media (DHM), the largest media company on the East End of Long Island, New York. Since joining the DHM team as Digital Director in 2011, he has overseen the launch of the industry-leading DansPapers.com, the redesign and growth of the flagship print product *Dan's Papers*—affectionately referred to as the "bible of the Hamptons" for the past six decades—and has been instrumental in launching and growing Dan's Taste of Summer, the largest food-and-wine event series on Long Island, as well as the award-winning *Behind the Hedges* magazine and website celebrating Hamptons real estate and luxury living. He served as CEO and Editorial Director at DHM from 2015 through 2017.

A graduate of the University of Pennsylvania, Eric began his career at the entertainment-publishing company TVSM, where he worked on a variety of print magazines and the launch of the first-ever TV-listings-based online property, TotalTV.com. He moved on to TV Guide Magazine Group, where he worked on developing products with brands ranging from HBO to NASCAR, as well as the launch of TVGuide.com. As a writer, he swam with sharks during Shark Week, cooked with Julia Child, threw batting practice to Hall of Famer Tony Gwynn, and has long championed the power of storytelling and the synergy of traditional and new media as a means to reaching an audience. He was Editor in Chief for *Inspire Your World*, the first national consumer magazine and website dedicated to volunteerism and philanthropy, and Executive Editor for the launch of OKMagazine.com, then joined the integrated marketing division of Meredith Corporation, where he led teams creating content-based products and programs for myriad clients, notably DIRECTV's *ACCESS* magazine.

Eric has also enjoyed time in front of the TV camera, as on-air talent for ESPN's daily morning show *Cold Pizza*, providing commentary on sports and pop culture, and covering events ranging from March Madness to the Democratic and Republican National Conventions. You may even catch a glimpse of him in ESPN's first TV movie, *A Season on the Brink*.

Eric lives on Long Island with his wife and daughter.

CPSIA information can be obtained
at www.ICGtesting.com
Printed in the USA
FFHW021742080519
52353239-57735FF

9 781733 016506